Pocket ATHENS

TOP SIGHTS • LOCAL LIFE • MADE EASY

Alexis Averbuck

In This Book

QuickStart Guide

Your keys to understanding the city – we help you decide what to do and how to do it

Need to Know
Tips for a smooth trip

Neighbourhoods
What's where

Explore Athens

The best things to see and do, neighbourhood by neighbourhood

Top Sights
Make the most of your visit

Local Life
The insider's city

The Best of Athens

The city's highlights in handy lists to help you plan

Best Walks
See the city on foot

Athens' Best...
The best experiences

Survival Guide

Tips and tricks for a seamless, hassle-free city experience

Getting Around
Travel like a local

Essential Information
Including where to stay

Our selection of the city's best places to eat, drink and experience:

◎ **Sights**

✕ **Eating**

🍷 **Drinking**

✦ **Entertainment**

🔒 **Shopping**

These symbols give you the vital information for each listing:

☏ Telephone Numbers
☉ Opening Hours
P Parking
⊘ Nonsmoking
@ Internet Access
🛜 Wi-Fi Access
🥗 Vegetarian Selection
📖 English-Language Menu

👪 Family-Friendly
🐾 Pet-Friendly
🚌 Bus
⛴ Ferry
M Metro
S Subway
🚊 Tram
🚉 Train

Find each listing quickly on maps for each neighbourhood:

Bar Hemingway

16 🍷 Map p233, B2

Legend has it that Hemi self, wielding a machine erate this timber-pan ered bar during showpiece is a en by Papa ar town. Dress s.com; Hôtel Rit ☉6.30pm-2a

---

Lonely Planet's Athens

Lonely Planet Pocket Guides are designed to get you straight to the heart of the city.

Inside you'll find all the must-see sights, plus tips to make your visit to each one really memorable. We've split the city into easy-to-navigate neighbourhoods and provided clear maps so you'll find your way around with ease. Our expert authors have searched out the best of the city: walks, food, nightlife and shopping, to name a few. Because you want to explore, our 'Local Life' pages will take you to some of the most exciting areas to experience the real Athens.

And of course you'll find all the practical tips you need for a smooth trip: itineraries for short visits, how to get around, and how much to tip the guy who serves you a drink at the end of a long day's exploration.

It's your guarantee of a really great experience.

Our Promise

You can trust our travel information because Lonely Planet authors visit the places we write about, each and every edition. We never accept freebies for positive coverage, so you can rely on us to tell it like it is.

QuickStart Guide 7

Explore Athens 21

Worth a Trip:

The Best of Athens 135

Athens' Best Walks

Athens' Best...

Survival Guide 157

QuickStart Guide

Welcome to Athens

From the iconic Acropolis rising majestically above the city to modern-art galleries, charming neighbourhood squares and lively bars, bustling Athens is a delightfully quirky clash of past and present, a city that confronts and surprises. Visitors are drawn by ancient monuments bathed in the famous light, but it's the city's infectious, creative vibe that enamours and enlivens.

View of the Parthenon and Acropolis (p24)
MFFOTO/SHUTTERSTOCK ©

Athens
Top Sights

Acropolis (p24)

The greatest symbol of the glory of ancient Greece, and a wonder of the world, the Acropolis (High City) rises spectacularly over Athens. Explore its magnificent Parthenon, the pinnacle of classical civilisation.

Acropolis Museum (p30)

Natural light cascades through the spacious galleries of the modern Acropolis Museum, illuminating the priceless treasures of the Acropolis. The museum's top-floor glass atrium presents the 161m-long Parthenon frieze in its entirety.

Ancient Agora (p40)

Follow in the footsteps of Socrates at the Ancient Agora, the heart of ancient Athens' civic life, and the birthplace of democracy. The Agora Museum bursts with unusual finds and the Temple of Hephaestus is exquisite.

National Archaeological Museum (p100)

Greece's preeminent museum houses the world's largest and finest collection of Greek antiquities. Priceless items date from the Neolithic Era (6800 BC) to the Cycladic, Mycenaean and Classical periods.

Temple of Olympian Zeus (p90)

Greece's largest temple took more than 700 years to build. Only a handful of its colossal columns remain at this mighty site, dedicated to Zeus and completed by the Roman Emperor Hadrian.

Keramikos (p124)

The city's ancient necropolis and ceremonial entrance is home to the impressive Street of Tombs and a superb small museum illustrating the splendour with which the ancient Greeks honoured their dead.

Filopappou Hill (p114)

The mythical battleground of Theseus and the Amazons is studded with ruins, has a charming Byzantine church and looks over the whole Attica basin, with splendid views of the Acropolis.

Benaki Museum (p76)

This excellent private museum shows the spectrum of Greece's historical and cultural development, and its fight for Independence. More than 20,000 pieces are displayed chronologically over four levels of a stunning neoclassical mansion.

Athens Local Life

Insider tips to help you find the real city

After visiting Athens' magnificent ancient wonders it's time to experience neighbourhood life in the city: we'll show you the way through the downtown hurly-burly to quiet shaded cafes and delightful neighbourhood squares, and guide you to Athenians' favourite dining haunts, shopping spots, galleries and bars.

Exploring Monastiraki (p44)

▶ Bustling markets
▶ Favourite hang-outs

Monastiraki's antique-lined squares and jam-packed pedestrian markets always draw Athenians, but new breeds of coffee shops, restaurants and bars have sprung up and attract a hip, young crowd.

Spend the day exploring the traditional and the trendy, manoeuvring through chaos and charm, grit and ancient splendour.

Wandering the Central Market (p56)

▶ Awesome people-watching
▶ Sensory extravaganzas

Athens' Central Market anchors a neighbourhood thrumming with activity and sensations. The market and its environs are an extravaganza of colours, scents and sounds comprising spice shops, tavernas, art galleries and the city's premier *rembetika* (blues songs) club.

Shopping Around Plaka (p60)

▶ Cool boutiques
▶ Top cocktails

Plaka – with its historic houses, Byzantine churches and winding narrow lanes climbing the slopes of the Acropolis – is much more than a tourist mecca. We'll show you how to shop like a local, and later head into Syntagma to find one of the city's most up-and-coming bar districts.

People-Watching in Kolonaki (p78)

▶ Thriving cafe scene
▶ Sizzling nightlife

Kolonaki is home to Athens' high society. Watch the world go by from its popular streetside cafes, top-notch contemporary-

Cafes, Kolonaki (p78)

rt galleries and favour-
e low-key tavernas.
hen pick between a
ght watching a film
nder the stars or club-
ng with the fashion-
ble set. Or do both!

Neighbourhood Life in Exarhia (p104)

▸ Graffiti-covered streets
▸ Lively restaurants and bars

eneath Exarhia's gritty
cade is one of Athens'
ost vibrant, unconven-
onal neighbourhoods.
reative graffiti shouts
ocial messages, and
w-key cafes around
ateia Exarhion show
s gentler side. Explore

its super, laid-back eateries and join its dynamic
student nightlife.

A Night Out in Keramikos & Gazi (p126)

▸ Gourmet dining
▸ Bars galore

Gazi and Keramikos
have become synony-
mous with partying at
an ever-changing array
of pubs and clubs.

Make a night of it
by dining at some of
Athens' top eateries
then exploring rooftop-
terrace cocktail bars or
the city's gay scene. Just
follow the party from
bar to bar.

Other great places to experience the city like a local:

Ancient
Promenade (p37)

Kalamaki
Kolonaki (p85)

Ariston (p68)

Kallipateira (p50)

Saturday Street
Market (p110)

Telis (p53)

Cremino (p66)

Cine
Athinaia (p86)

Rembetika
Istoria (p111)

Athens
Day Planner

Day One

Start with an early-morning climb through Plaka's streets to the glorious **Acropolis** (p24), going early to beat the crowds and the heat. Then wind your way down through the **Ancient Agora** (p40), the centre of ancient Athens' civic life. Venture into the streets of Plaka and Monastiraki, passing by the **Roman Agora** (p48) with its unusual **Tower of the Winds** (p48), before heading to Monastiraki's souvlaki hub to initiate yourself with a *gyros* (meat slithers cooked on a vertical rotisserie, usually eaten with pitta bread) at **Thanasis** (p52), or have an excellent meal at sweet **Café Avyssinia** (p51).

Explore the **Monastiraki Flea Market** (p45) or shop for souvenirs in **Plaka** (p60), then head to the **Acropolis Museum** (p30) to see the Parthenon masterpieces. Visit the **Theatre of Dionysos** (p28) and **Odeon of Herodes Atticus** (p28) if you didn't see them while you were at the Acropolis.

Dine under the floodlit Acropolis at **Strofi** (p35) or **Dionysos** (p115), then head to the best bars in Monastiraki and Syntagma, such as **Tailor Made** (p45) on Plateia Agia Irini or the multitude of venues near Plateia Karytsi, such as **Gin Joint** (p61).

Day Two

Watch the *evzones* (guards) strut their high-kicking stuff during the **changing of the guard** (p64) ceremony outside Parliament in Plateia Syntagmatos. Then head to the **Benaki Museum** (p76) for its extensive collections tracing Greek culture over millennia. In summer lunch alfresco on its terrace overlooking the National Gardens; in winter stay cosy inside the wraparound windows.

Stroll down through the **National Gardens** (p64) to the old **Panathenaic Stadium** (p94) and then to the **Temple of Olympian Zeus** (p90) and **Hadrian's Arch** (p91). Afterwards, peruse Greece's most significant antiquities at the **National Archaeological Museum** (p100), then head to bohemian **Exarhia** (p104) for an afternoon drink or an early meal.

Take the funicular railway up **Lykavittos Hill** (p79) at sunset for impressive panoramic views of Athens and have dinner in Kolonaki at **Oikeio** (p79) or one of its many other fine restaurants, followed by a nightcap at **Rock'n'Roll** (p79) or **Mai Tai** (p86). Alternatively, make your way to Gazi to dine at one of its mod tavernas, such as **Kanella** (p130), and sip terrace-top drinks at a popular hot spot like **Gazarte** (p127), before bar-hopping till dawn.

ort on time?

e've arranged Athens' must-sees into these day-by-day itineraries to make sure
u see the very best of the city in the time you have available.

ay Three

Wander the wild **Athens Central Market** (p56) and the teeming reets around it, and stock up on food d drink to take home – such as this ar's olive oil. Then have lunch at a l-world taverna nearby: try **Diporto ɣoras** (p57).

Make your way to Kolonaki for high-end window-shopping or ople-watching at its trendy cafes, and en get a dose of culture at the **Museum Cycladic Art** (p83) and the **Byzantine Christian Museum** (p82) with **Aristo-'s Lyceum** (p82) next door. Or head to e Syngrou area for the new **National useum of Contemporary Art** (p33) in converted brewery.

Dine in the centre at **Tzitzikas & Mermingas** (p67) for mezed- s (appetisers) or **2 Mazi** (p67) for editerranean fare with flair, then watch noonlit movie at one of Athens' outdoor emas such as **Aigli Cinema** (p97), ne Paris (p70) or **Thission** (p121). catch live local music at a *rembetika* ues songs) club in winter, such as **Stoa hanaton** (p57). If it's summer, check ograms for festivals and small venues luding the **Half Note Jazz Club** (p96), hit a music taverna in Plaka, such as ordeon** (p51), or in Psyrri.

Day Four

Use the morning to immerse yourself in the **Keramikos** (p124) site with its grand Street of Tombs and small museum full of masterpieces. Then meander over to the **Museum of Islamic Art** (p129) for its superb collection spanning centuries. Lunch in Monastiraki at **Kuzina** (p136) or in Psyrri at **Ivis** (p52) or **Nikitas** (p52).

Then, take a long walk or quick cab ride to the **Benaki Museum Pireos Annexe** (p129) for the latest contemporary art in a cool industrial building. Or take a stroll along the **pedestrian promenade** (p37), climbing **Filopappou Hill** (p114) for the views, then winding back to the cafes around Thisio.

If you've booked ahead, dine at one of Athens' top spots, including **Funky Gourmet** (p126) or **Spondi** (p95). Also plan ahead and get tickets for the **Odeon of Herodes Atticus** (p28) or **Megaron Mousikis** (p34) to see one of the city's grand theatre and musical venues in action. Alternatively, swing into one of Athens' new trendsetting spaces, which are equal parts gallery, cafe, bar and theatre: **Taf** (p51), **Six DOGS** (p45) or **Bios** (p127). Or, if it's summer, make the adventurous detour off-map to Glyfada's beach nightclubs.

Need to Know

For more information, see Survival Guide (p157).

Currency
Euro (€).

Language
Greek.

Visas
Not required for citizens of the EU or Schengen countries; not required for stays of up to 90 days for citizens of the US, Canada, Australia and New Zealand.

Money
ATMs widely available. Credit cards accepted in many hotels, restaurants and shops, but not all.

Mobile Phones
Local SIM cards can be used in European and Australian phones. Most other phones can be set to roaming. US/Canadian phones need to have a dual- or tri-band system.

Time
Eastern European Time (GMT/UTC plus two hours).

Plugs & Adaptors
Plugs have two round pins; electrical current is 220–240V. North American visitors will require an adaptor and a transformer.

Tipping
Small change and rounding up is customary.

① Before You Go

Your Daily Budget

Budget less than €100
▶ Dorm beds €25, pension doubles from €
▶ Eat at souvlaki shops and tavernas
▶ Save euros in the shoulder or low seasor

Midrange €100–200
▶ Doubles in midrange hotels €80–160
▶ Local tavernas have hearty midrange fare
▶ Most sights have reasonable entrance fee

Top End more than €200
▶ Double rooms in top hotels from €150
▶ Excellent dining; some accompanied by Michelin stars
▶ Nightlife and cocktail bars abound

Useful Websites

Athens' Official Site (www.thisisathens.org) With what's-on listings.

Arts & Culture (www.elculture.gr) Theatre, music and cinema listings.

Ministry of Culture (www.culture.gr) Museums and archaeological sites.

Greek National Tourism Organisation (www.visitgreece.gr)

Lonely Planet (www.lonelyplanet.com/ Greece/Athens) Destination information, hotel bookings, traveller forum.

Advance Planning

Three months before Reserve your hotel early to increase choice and reduce price.

One month before Book tickets for a perfo mance at Odeon of Herodes Atticus (p28) Megaron Mousikis (p34). Reserve a table a top-end restaurants.

One week before Check online for strike information (http://livingingreece.gr/ strikes); book tours.

2 Arriving in Athens

st visitors arrive at Athens' Eleftherios
nizelos International Airport at Spata,
km east of the city centre. See p160 for
ore information. Most ferries and cruises
ive at the port of Piraeus.

From Eleftherios Venizelos
ternational Airport

estination	Best Transport
yntagma & Plaka	metro (blue line); express bus X95
onastiraki	metro (blue line)
hisio	metro (blue line to green line)
olonaki	metro (blue line); express bus X95
akrygianni	metro (blue line to red line)
syrri	metro (blue line)

From Piraeus Port

estination	Best Transport
yntagma & Plaka	metro (green line to blue line); bus 040
onastiraki	metro (green line)
hisio	metro (green line)
olonaki	metro (green line to blue line)
akrygianni	metro (green line to red line)
syrri	metro (green line)

3 Getting Around

Athens has an extensive and inexpensive
integrated public-transport network of buses,
metro, trolleybuses and trams. Pick up maps
and timetables at the EOT tourist office,
(p165) the airport or online at www.oasa.gr.

The metro (www.amel.gr) is the best way
to get around town. Conveniently, all public
transport operates under the same ticketing
system. Tickets good for 70 minutes (€1.20)
and a 24-hour/five-day travel pass (€4/10)
are valid for all forms of public transport
except for airport services (airport metro €8,
bus €5).

The three-day tourist pass (€20) includes
one airport round trip.

 Metro

Three colour-coded lines criss-cross central
Athens. Line 1 (green) also serves Piraeus.
Line 2 (red) gets the closest to the Acropolis
and the Acropolis Museum. Line 3 (blue)
serves the airport, and at the time of writing
was being extended to Piraeus. The central
hubs are Syntagma (blue and red lines) and
Monastiraki (blue and green lines).

 Bus, Trolleybus & Tram

Blue-and-white local express buses, regular
buses and electric trolleybuses operate every
15 minutes from 5am to midnight. They are
generally slower than the metro, and best for
neighbourhoods outside the centre. The free
OASA map shows most routes.

Athens' tram (www.stasy.gr) offers a slow,
scenic coastal journey to Faliro and Voula,
via Glyfada.

 Taxi

Avoid driving in Athens at all costs – it is
much simpler and cheaper to take a cab, but
beware of taxi-driver scams. Fixed fares to/
from the airport are posted at the airport
taxi stand; expect day/night (midnight to
5am) €35/50 to the city centre, and €47/72
to Piraeus.

Athens
Neighbourhoods

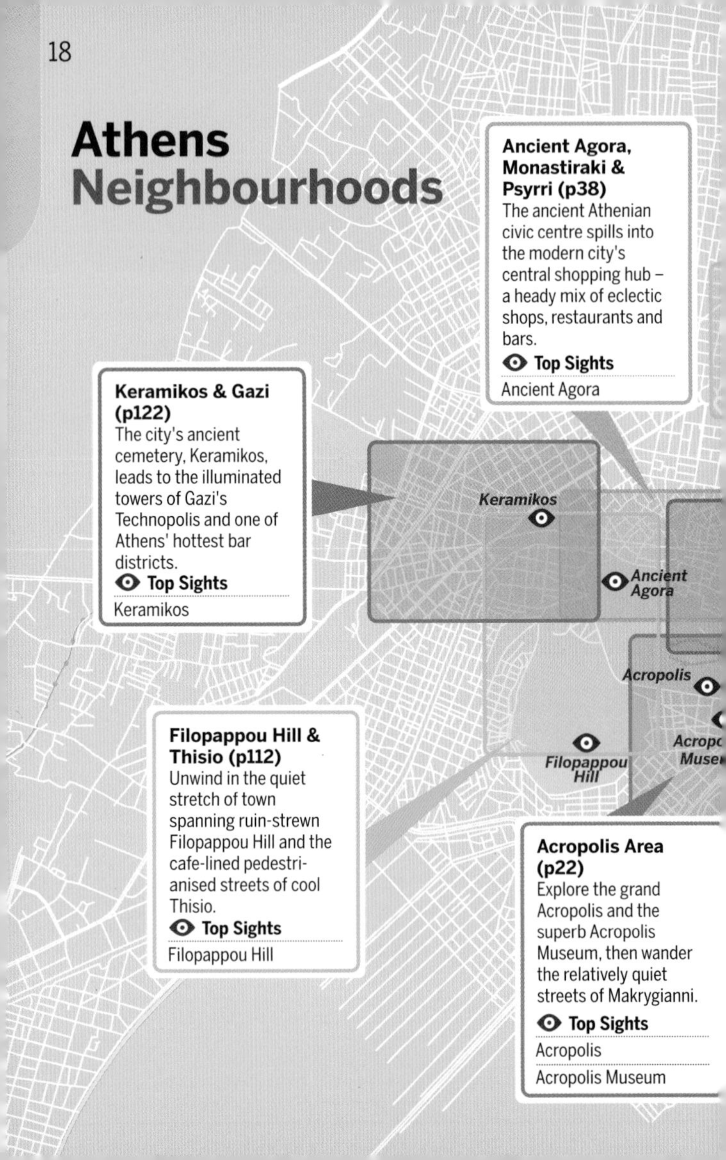

Ancient Agora, Monastiraki & Psyrri (p38)
The ancient Athenian civic centre spills into the modern city's central shopping hub – a heady mix of eclectic shops, restaurants and bars.
⊙ Top Sights
Ancient Agora

Keramikos & Gazi (p122)
The city's ancient cemetery, Keramikos, leads to the illuminated towers of Gazi's Technopolis and one of Athens' hottest bar districts.
⊙ Top Sights
Keramikos

Keramikos
⊙

⊙ Ancient Agora

Acropolis ⊙

Filopappou Hill & Thisio (p112)
Unwind in the quiet stretch of town spanning ruin-strewn Filopappou Hill and the cafe-lined pedestrianised streets of cool Thisio.
⊙ Top Sights
Filopappou Hill

Acrop
Muse

Filopappou
Hill
⊙

Acropolis Area (p22)
Explore the grand Acropolis and the superb Acropolis Museum, then wander the relatively quiet streets of Makrygianni.
⊙ Top Sights
Acropolis
Acropolis Museum

**National Archaeo-
logical Museum &
Exarhia (p98)**
Discover the treasures
at the world's foremost
collection of Greek art
and antiquities, then
soak up the vibe in
bohemian Exarhia.

👁 **Top Sights**
National Archaeological
Museum

**Benaki Museum &
Kolonaki (p74)**
Consistently fashionable
and loaded with popular
boutiques, cafes and
bars, Kolonaki is also
home to some of the
city's premier museums,
including the Benaki.

👁 **Top Sights**
Benaki Museum

**Greek Parliament,
Syntagma & Plaka
(p58)**
Parliament anchors
enormous Plateia
Syntagmatos, and the
winding lanes of Plaka,
lined with shops,
become quaintly
residential as they twist
up the slope of the
Acropolis.

**Temple of
Olympian Zeus &
Panathenaic
Stadium (p88)**
The colossal temple
leads to the stadium,
the home of the first
modern Olympic games,
and laid-back residential
neighbourhoods Mets
and Pangrati.

👁 **Top Sights**
Temple of Olympian
Zeus

*National
Archaeological
Museum*

*Benaki
Museum*
👁

*Temple of
Olympian
Zeus*
👁

Explore
Athens

Worth a Trip

Entrance, Acropolis (p24)
ED FREEMAN/GETTY IMAGES ©

Explore

Acropolis Area

Athens' crown jewel is the Acropolis (pictured, above). This epic monument stands over the city, and on its southern slopes a fabulous modern museum holds its treasures in spacious splendour. The promenade between the Acropolis and the Acropolis Museum bustles with tourists and strolling families. Despite its proximity to the centre, the quiet neighbourhood of Makrygianni, south of the Acropolis, is refreshingly untouristy.

The Sights in a Day

☀ Start as early as you can manage to make your way to the Acropolis and beat the heat and the crowds. Explore the hill top first, from the **Parthenon** (p25) to the resplendent **Caryatids** (p27) at the **Erechtheion** (p26) and the precious **Temple of Athena Nike** (p27). Wander down the Acropolis' southern slope to take in the **Odeon of Herodes Atticus** (p28), the **Stoa of Eumenes** (p28) and the **Theatre of Dionysos** (p28).

☀ Grab a bite to eat at the super-scenic and relaxing **Acropolis Museum** (p30) cafe-restaurant before taking plenty of time to peruse the thousands of works in the collection. You can examine everything from tiny coins to magnificent pedimental sculptures, all arrayed beautifully in the modern (air-conditioned!) building. The movie on the top floor makes a nice break too.

☾ If there's any time left before dinner, check out neighbourhood shops such as contemporary jewellery and art gallery **El.Marneri Galerie** (p37), or take a short stroll along the **Ancient Promenade** (p37), listening to the buskers. Plan to dine out at one of the area's fine restaurants, such as **Mani Mani** (p35), **Strofi** (p35) or **Dionysos** (p36), and then hit **Duende** (p36), **Sfika** (p36) or **Tiki Athens** (p36) for a nightcap.

👁 Top Sights

Acropolis (p24)

Acropolis Museum (p30)

🖤 Best of Athens

Archaeological Sites

Acropolis (p24)

Theatre of Dionysos (p28)

Odeon of Herodes Atticus (p28)

Museums

Acropolis Museum (p30)

Food

Mani Mani (p35)

Getting There

Ⓜ**Metro** The metro is the best option. Akropoli station (red line) sits near the Acropolis Museum at the base of the Acropolis hill, just off the major boulevard Leoforos Syngrou. Arriving at Syntagma station (blue and red lines) or Monastiraki station (blue and green lines), to the west of the Acropolis hill, allows for a leisurely walk through Plaka's winding lanes to the Acropolis' western entrance.

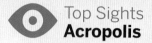

Top Sights
Acropolis

The Acropolis is the most important ancient site in the Western world. Crowned by the Parthenon, it rises over Athens, visible from almost everywhere within the city. Its monuments of Pentelic marble gleam white in the midday sun and gradually take on a honey hue as the sun sinks, while at night they stand brilliantly illuminated above the city. A glimpse of this magnificent sight cannot fail to exalt your spirit.

👁 Map p32, B1

📞 210 321 0219, disabled access 📞 210 321 4172

http://odysseus.culture.gr

adult/child/concession €12/free/6

🕐 8am-8pm Apr-Oct, to 5pm Nov-Mar, last entry 30min before closing

Ⓜ Akropoli

Parthenon

Don't Miss

Parthenon

The Parthenon is the monument that epitomises the glory of Ancient Greece. It is dedicated to Athena Parthenos, the goddess embodying the power and prestige of the city. The largest Doric temple ever completed in Greece, and the only one built completely of Pentelic marble (apart from the wood in its roof), it was designed by Iktinos and Kallicrates to be the preeminent monument of the Acropolis and was completed in time for the Great Panathenaic Festival of 438 BC.

Parthenon Columns

The eight fluted Doric columns at either end and 17 on each side were ingeniously curved to create an optical illusion: the foundations (like all the 'horizontal' surfaces of the temple) are slightly concave and the columns are slightly convex making both appear straight. Supervised by Pheidias, the sculptors Agoracritos and Alcamenes worked on the architectural sculptures of the Parthenon, including the pediments, frieze and metopes, which were brightly coloured and gilded.

Parthenon Pediments

The temple's pediments (the triangular elements topping the east and west facades) were filled with elaborately carved three-dimensional sculptures. The west side depicted Athena and Poseidon in their contest for the city's patronage, the east Athena's birth from Zeus' head. See their remnants and the rest of the Acropolis' sculptures and artefacts in the Acropolis Museum.

Metopes & Frieze

The Parthenon's metopes, designed by Pheidias, are square carved panels set between channelled triglyphs. The metopes on the eastern side

---

☑ Top Tips

▶ Visit early in the morning to escape the crowds and heat.

▶ The main entrance is from Dionysiou Areopagitou near the Odeon of Herodes Atticus.

▶ Wheelchairs access the site via a cage lift; call ahead to arrange it (📞210 321 4172) then go to the main entrance.

▶ Large bags must be left at the main entrance cloakroom.

▶ The Acropolis admission pass (p35) includes entry to several sights.

▶ Box offices close 15 to 90 minutes before sites. Check www.culture.gr for free-admission holidays and changing opening hours.

✗ Take a Break

Swing into Dionysos (p36) for coffee and excellent views of the monument.

Or, book ahead for a late-afternoon lunch at Mani Mani (p35).

depicted the Olympian gods fighting the giants, and on the western side they showed Theseus leading the Athenian youths into battle against the Amazons. The southern metopes illustrated the contest of the Lapiths and centaurs at a marriage feast, while the northern ones depicted the sacking of Troy. The internal cella was topped by the Ionic frieze, a continuous sculptured band depicting the Panathenaic Procession.

Statue of Athena Polias

The statue for which the temple was built – the Athena Polias (Athena of the City) – was considered one of the wonders of the ancient world. It was taken to Constantinople in AD 426, where it disappeared. Designed by Pheidias and completed in 432 BC, it stood almost 12m high on its pedestal and was plated in gold. Athena's face, hands and feet were made of ivory, and the eyes fashioned from jewels.

Erechtheion

The Erechtheion, completed around 406 BC, was a sanctuary built on the most sacred part of the Acropolis: the spot where Poseidon struck the ground with his trident, and where Athena produced the olive tree. Named after Erechtheus, a mythical king of Athens, the temple housed the cults of Athena, Poseidon and Erechtheus. This supreme example of Ionic architecture was ingeniously built on several levels to counteract the uneven bedrock.

Acropolis

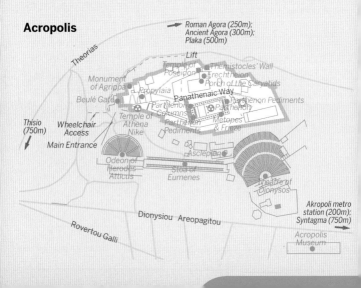

Porch of the Caryatids

The Erechtheion is immediately recognisable by the six majestic maiden columns, the Caryatids (415 BC), that support its southern portico. Modelled on women from Karyai (modern-day Karyes, in Lakonia), each maiden is thought to have held a libation bowl in one hand, and to be drawing up her dress with the other. Those you see are plaster casts. The originals (except for one removed by Lord Elgin, now in the British Museum) are in the Acropolis Museum (p30).

Temple of Poseidon

Though he didn't win patronage of the city, Poseidon was worshipped on the northern side of the Erechtheion. The porch still bears the mark of his trident-strike. Imagine the finely decorated coffered porch painted in rich colours, as it was before.

Themistocles' Wall

Crafty general Themistocles (524–459 BC) hastened to build a protective wall around the Acropolis and in so doing incorporated elements from archaic temples on the site. Look for the column drums built into the wall on the north side of the Erechtheion.

Propylaia

The monumental entrance to the Acropolis, the Propylaia was built by Mnesicles between 437 BC and 432 BC and consists of a central hall with two wings on either side. In ancient times its five gates were the only entrances to the 'upper city'. The middle gate

DAVID BUFFINGTON/GETTY IMAGES ©

Porch of the Caryatids

opens onto the Panathenaic Way. The ceiling of the central hall was painted with gold stars on a dark-blue background. The northern wing was used as a *pinakothiki* (art gallery).

Temple of Athena Nike

Recently restored, this exquisitely proportioned tiny Pentelic marble temple was designed by Kallicrates and built around 425 BC. The internal cella housed a wooden statue of Athena as Victory (Nike) and the exterior friezes illustrated scenes from mythology, the Battle of Plataea (479 BC) and Athenians fighting Boeotians and Persians. Parts of the frieze are in the Acropolis

Museum, as are some relief sculptures, including the beautiful depiction of Athena Nike fastening her sandal.

Beulé Gate & Monument of Agrippa

Just outside the Propylaia lies the Beulé Gate, named after French archaeologist Ernest Beulé, who uncovered it in 1852. The 8m pedestal halfway up the zigzagging ramp to the Propylaia was once topped by the *Monument of Agrippa*. This bronze statue of the Roman general riding a chariot was erected in 27 BC to commemorate victory in the Panathenaic Games.

Theatre of Dionysos

Originally, a 6th-century-BC timber **theatre** (📞210 322 4625; Dionysiou Areopagitou; adult/child €2/free, with Acropolis pass free; 🕑8am-8pm, reduced hours low season; Ⓜ Akropoli) was built here, on the site of the Festival of the Great Dionysia. During Athens' golden age, the theatre hosted productions of the works of Aeschylus, Sophocles, Euripides and Aristophanes. Reconstructed in stone and marble between 342 and 326 BC, the theatre held 17,000 spectators (spread over 64 tiers, of which only about 20 tiers survive) and an altar to Dionysos in the orchestra pit.

Theatre of Dionysos Thrones & Carvings

The ringside Pentelic marble thrones were for dignitaries and priests. The grandest, with lions' paws, satyrs and griffins, was reserved for the Priest of Dionysos. The 2nd-century-BC reliefs at the rear of the stage depict the exploits of Dionysos. The two hefty men (who still have their heads) are *selini*, worshippers of the mythical Selinos, the debauched father of the satyrs, whose favourite pastime was charging up mountains with his oversized phallus in lecherous pursuit of nymphs.

Asclepion & Stoa of Eumenes

Above the Theatre of Dionysos, steps lead to the Asclepion, a temple built around a sacred spring. The worship of Asclepius, the physician son of Apollo, began in Epidavros and was introduced to Athens in 429 BC at a time when plague was sweeping the city: people sought cures here.

Beneath the Asclepion, the Stoa of Eumenes is a colonnade built by Eumenes II, king of Pergamum (197–159 BC), as a shelter and promenade for theatre audiences.

Odeon of Herodes Atticus

The path continues west from the Asclepion to the magnificent **Odeon of Herodes Atticus** (📞210 324 1807; Ⓜ Akropoli), known as the Herodion. It was built in AD 161 by wealthy Roman Herodes Atticus in memory of his wife Regilla. The theatre was excavated in 1857–58 and completely restored between 1950 and 1961. Performances of drama, music and dance are held here during the **Athens Festival** (📞210 322 1459; www.hellenicfestival.gr).

Understand

The Acropolis

Contest for Athens

After Kekrops, a Phoenician, founded a city on a huge rock near the sea, the gods of Olympus proclaimed that it should be named after the deity who could provide the most valuable legacy for mortals. Athena (goddess of wisdom, among other things) produced an olive tree, symbol of peace and prosperity. Poseidon (god of the sea) struck a rock with his trident and a saltwater spring emerged (some versions say he made a horse). The gods judged that Athena's gift would better serve the citizens of Athens with nourishment, oil and wood. To this day the goddess dominates Athens' mythology and the city's great monuments are dedicated to her.

Building the Acropolis

The Acropolis was first inhabited in neolithic times (4000–3000 BC). The first temples were built during the Mycenaean era in homage to the goddess Athena. People lived on the Acropolis until the late 6th century BC, but in 510 BC the Delphic Oracle declared that it should be the province of the gods.

After all the buildings on the Acropolis were reduced to ashes by the Persians on the eve of the Battle of Salamis (480 BC), Pericles set about an ambitious rebuilding program. He transformed the Acropolis into a city of temples, now regarded as the zenith of classical Greek achievement. He spared no expense: only the best materials, architects, sculptors and artists were good enough for a city dedicated to the cult of Athena. The city was a showcase of lavishly coloured colossal buildings and of gargantuan statues, some of bronze, others of marble plated with gold and encrusted with precious stones.

Preserving the Site

The temples suffered under years of foreign occupation, including a 1687 explosion of Turkish gunpowder being stored in the Parthenon, which damaged all of the buildings. Foreign archaeologists pilfered material, including Lord Elgin who in 1801 spirited away a vast collection of Acropolis sculptures, which now reside in the British Museum despite Greece's demands for their return. Inept renovations following Independence, earthquakes and, more recently, pollution added to the site's woes. Restoration is ongoing.

Top Sights
Acropolis Museum

The grand modernist Acropolis Museum at the southern foot of the Acropolis displays the monument's surviving treasures. While the collection covers the Archaic and Roman periods, the emphasis is on the Acropolis of the 5th century BC, considered the apotheosis of Greece's artistic achievement. The spectacular museum cleverly showcases layers of history: subterranean ruins are visible below, and the Acropolis rises above, thus allowing visitors to see the masterpieces in context.

👁 Map p32, C3

📞 210 900 0901

www.theacropolismuseum.gr

Dionysiou Areopagitou 15, Makrygianni

adult/child €5/free

🕐 8am-4pm Mon, to 8pm Tue-Sun, to 10pm Fri, hours change Nov-Mar

Ⓜ Akropoli

Don't Miss

Archaic Gallery

Bathed in natural light, the 1st floor is a veritable forest of statues, mostly offerings to Athena. These include stunning examples of 6th-century *kore* (maiden) statues: young women in draped clothing and elaborate braids. The 570 BC youth bearing a calf is one of the rare male statues discovered.

Early Temple Treasures

The Archaic Gallery also houses bronze figurines and finds from temples pre-dating the Parthenon, which were destroyed by the Persians. Elaborate pedimental sculptures include Heracles slaying the Lernaian Hydra and a lioness devouring a bull.

Parthenon Gallery

The museum's crowning glory, this top-floor glass atrium built in alignment with the Parthenon showcases the Parthenon's pediments, metopes and 160m frieze. For the first time in over 200 years, the frieze is displayed in sequence, depicting the Panathenaic Procession. Interspersed between golden-hued originals are white plaster replicas of missing pieces.

Caryatids

Five grand Caryatids, the world-famous maiden columns that held up the porch of the Erechtheion, rule the mezzanine (the sixth is in the British Museum). Nearby, find a giant floral *akrotirion* (decorative element at the end of a classical building's gable) that once crowned the southern ridge of the Parthenon pediment.

Foyer Gallery

Finds from the slopes of the Acropolis fill the entryway gallery. The glass floor allows glimpses of the ruins below. More recent objects found in excavations of the settlement include two clay statues of Nike.

☑ Top Tips

▶ Beneath the entrance look for the ruins of an ancient Athenian neighbourhood, which have been deftly incorporated into the museum design after being uncovered during excavations.

▶ Allow time for the fine museum shop (ground floor) and the movie describing the history of the Acropolis (top floor).

▶ Last admission is a half hour before closing, and galleries are cleared 15 minutes before closing.

▶ If you are under 18 or a student, bring ID for free admission. EU citizens who are over 65 also enter free with ID.

✕ Take a Break

The museum's cafe-restaurant on the 2nd floor has superb views across the way to the Acropolis, and prices are surprisingly reasonable (mains €10 to €15). Eat inside or sip a coffee alfresco on the terrace.

Areopagus
3 Hill

Theorias

Acropolis

PLAKA

Thespidos
Afroditis

Shelley
Galanou

Epimenidou

Thrasyllou

Vakhou

Vyronos

Frynihou

Eschinou

Dionysiou Areopagitou

7

Webster

6

Ilias Lalaounis 2
Jewellery
Museum

Kallisperi

MAKRYGIANNI

9

Makri

Tzireon

4

Rovertou Galli

Kallisperi

Atelier Spyros
Vassiliou

Fratti

Galli

Entrance

Karyatidon

**Acropolis
Museum**

Akropoli

Diakou Ath

Filopappou
Hill

Promahou

Kavalloti

Hatzihristou

Parinou

16

Lembesi

8

Garivaldi

Kavalloti

Erehthiou

Zitrou

15

Diakou Ath

Propyleon

Parthenos

Petmeza

Strateon

13

14

Mouson

Drakou

Tsami Karatasou

10

5

12

Vourvahi

Lossif Roc

Liakou

Veikou

Dimitrakopoulou N

Falirou

Petmeza

Nakou Koryz

Dikeou

Gioni

Markou Botsari

11

S Kontouli

Kallirrois

Leof Andreas Syngrou

Plateia Ag
Pandeleimonos

Zaharitsa

Z Botsari Noti

Plateia
Gargarettas

Drakou

Sismani

Iras

Botsari Tousa

Alkimou

Plateia
Kynosargous

Veikou

Inglesi

Theokritou

Aglaoni

Falirou

**Syngrou-
Fix**

Iras

Iymfristou

Evdohou

Theono

Sehou D

Irakleous

Kiada

1 National
Museum of
Contemporary Art

Fotomara

Ekateou

200 m
0.1 miles

National Museum of Contemporary Art

Sights

National Museum of Contemporary Art
MUSEUM

1 ◉ Map p32, B5

In 2015 this museum inaugurated spectacularly renovated quarters at the former Fix Brewery on Leoforos Syngrou. It shows top-notch rotating exhibitions of Greek and international contemporary art. Its permanent exhibitions include paintings, installations, photography, video and new media, as well as experimental architecture. (☏210 924 2111; www.emst.gr; Kallirrois & Frantzi, Koukaki-Syngrou; adult/child €3/free; ⊗11am-7pm Tue, Wed & Fri-Sun, to 10pm Thu; Ⓜ Syngrou-Fix)

Ilias Lalaounis Jewellery Museum
MUSEUM

2 ◉ Map p32, B2

Jewellery and decorative arts inspired by various periods in Greek history showcase the talents of Greece's renowned jeweller Ilias Lalaounis. The museum demonstrates techniques from prehistoric times. The permanent collection includes thematic displays of more than 4000 pieces of jewellery and intricate microsculptures designed by Lalaounis since the 1940s. The museum also hosts temporary exhibitions and runs cultural programs dedicated to the art. (☏210 922 1044; www.lalaounis-jewelrymuseum.gr; Kallisperi 12, cnr Karyatidon, Makrygianni; adult/child €5/3; ⊗9am-3pm Tue-Sat, 11am-4pm Sun; Ⓜ Akropoli)

Understand

Birthplace of Theatre

The Festival of the Great Dionysia

The tyrant Peisistratos introduced the annual Festival of the Great Dionysia during the 6th century BC, and held it in the world's first theatre on the south slope of the Acropolis. During the festival masses of people attended contests where men clad in goatskins sang and danced, followed by feasting and revelry. Drama as we know it dates back to these contests. At one of them, Thespis left the ensemble and took centre stage for a solo performance, an act considered to be the first true dramatic performance – hence the term 'thespian'.

Drama in the Golden Age

During the golden age in the 5th century BC, the festival was one of the state's major events. Politicians sponsored dramas by writers such as Aeschylus, Sophocles and Euripides, with lighter relief provided by the bawdy comedies of Aristophanes. People came from all over Attica, with their expenses met by the state.

In Roman times the theatre was also used for performances and state events.

Greek Theatre Today

The works of the ancient Greek playwrights, as well as more 'modern' plays and operas, are still performed in the few surviving ancient theatres during summer festivals, such as the **Hellenic Festival** (Athens & Epidavros Festival; www.greekfestival.gr; ☺Jun-Aug). The most notable of these are the Odeon of Herodes Atticus (p28) and the stunningly preserved theatre in Epidavros in the Peloponnese.

Athens also supports a lively winter theatre tradition, with more than 200 theatres (more than any other European city) presenting anything from Sophocles to Beckett and works by contemporary Greek playwrights. The **Megaron Mousikis** (Athens Concert Hall; ☎210 728 2333; www.megaron.gr; Kokkali 1, cnr Leoforos Vasilissis Sofias, Ilissia; ☺box office 10am-6pm Mon-Fri, to 2pm Sat, later on performance days; Ⓜ Megaro Mousikis) is the modern symphony hall, and the **National Theatre** (☎210 528 8100; www.n-t.gr; Agiou Konstantinou 22-24) is in the Omonia neighbourhood.

Areopagus Hill
PARK

3 ⊙ Map p32, A1

This rocky outcrop below the Acropolis has great views over the Ancient Agora. According to mythology, it was here that Ares was tried by the council of the gods for the murder of Halirrhothios, son of Poseidon. The council accepted his defence of justifiable deicide on the grounds that he was protecting his daughter, Alcippe, from unwanted advances. (Ⓜ Monastiraki)

Atelier Spyros Vassiliou
ART GALLERY

4 ⊙ Map p32, A2

The home and studio of leading 20th-century Greek painter and set designer Spyros Vassiliou (1902–1985) has been converted into an impressive museum and archive of his work. Exhibits include his celebrated paintings depicting urban Athens, theatre sets, his artist's tools and illustrations from literary journals and newspapers. Temporary exhibitions, too. (☎210 923 1502; www.spyrosvassiliou.org; Webster 5a, Makrygianni; adult/child €4/2; ⏰10am-6pm Tue, Fri & Sat, noon-6pm Wed, 10am-6pm Sun, closed Jul & Aug, reduced hours Nov-Apr; Ⓜ Akropoli)

Eating

Mani Mani
REGIONAL GREEK €€

5 ✕ Map p32, C3

Head upstairs to the relaxing, cheerful dining rooms of this delightful modern restaurant, which specialises in regional cuisine from Mani in the Peloponnese. Standouts include the ravioli with Swiss chard (silverbeet), chervil and cheese, and the tangy Mani sausage with orange. Almost all dishes can be ordered as half portions (at half-price), allowing you to sample widely. (☎210 921 8180; www.manimani.com.gr; Falirou 10, Makrygianni; mains €9-15; ⏰2-11pm, closed Jul & Aug; Ⓜ Akropoli)

Strofi
GREEK €€

6 ✕ Map p32, A2

Book ahead for a Parthenon view from the rooftop of this exquisitely renovated townhouse. Food is simple Greek, but

☑ Top Tip

Acropolis Pass

The €12 Acropolis admission includes entry to Athens' main ancient sites: Ancient Agora, Roman Agora, Hadrian's Library, Keramikos, the Temple of Olympian Zeus and the Theatre of Dionysos. The ticket is valid for four days; otherwise individual site fees apply. Usually, similar opening hours (8am to 8pm April to October, 8.30am to 3pm November to March) apply for all of these sites, but it pays to double-check as hours fluctuate from year to year. Enter the sites free on the first Sunday of the month from November to March, and on certain holidays.

the setting, with elegant white linen and sweet service, elevates the experience to romantic levels. (📞210 921 4130; www.strofi.gr; Rovertou Galli 25, Makrygianni; mains €11-15; 🕓noon-1am; Ⓜ Akropoli)

Dionysos

MEDITERRANEAN €€€

7 ✕ Map p32, A2

Location, location, location. Eat here for the fantastic sweep of plate glass looking out onto the unblemished south slope of the Acropolis. Food is pricey but service is attentive... Date night? (📞210 923 1936; www.dionysoszonars.gr; Rovertou Galli 43, Makrygianni; mains €19-36; 🕓restaurant noon-1am, cafe 8am-1am; Ⓜ Akropoli)

Aglio, Olio & Peperoncino

ITALIAN €€

8 ✕ Map p32, D3

Hardly the most obvious place for a restaurant, but this hidden gem on a side-street near the Acropolis metro stop is a great choice for no-frills classic Italian pastas and a cosy, trattoria ambience. (📞210 921 1801; Porinou 13, Makrygianni; mains €15-25; 🕓8pm-12.45am Tue-Sat, 2-6.45pm Sun; Ⓜ Akropoli)

Fresko Yogurt Bar

YOGHURT €

9 ✕ Map p32, D2

Delicious fresh Greek yoghurt is the base of all things here. Either fresh or in smoothie form, you can pair it with any number of toppings, from chocolatey to black-cherry spoon sweets. A perfect cool-off after seeing the Acropolis. (📞210 923 3760; www.freskoyogurtbar.gr;

Dionysiou Areopagitou 3, Makrygianni; yoghurt from €2.20; 🕓9am-9pm; Ⓜ Akropoli)

Lotte Cafe-Bistrot

CAFE €

10 ✕ Map p32, C3

This small, charming cafe is decked out with vintage books and tea sets, and has bistro tables lining the footpath. Food tends towards cakes and light snacks. (📞211 407 8639; Tsami Karatsou 2, Makrygianni; snacks €2.50-7; 🕓9am-9pm; Ⓜ Akropoli)

Drinking

Duende

BAR

This intimate pub feels almost like a Parisian brasserie and is tucked away on a quiet side street (see 9 ✕ Map p32, D2). It's best for wine and whiskey, not cocktails or food. (Tzireon 2, Makrygianni; 🕓8pm-3am; Ⓜ Akropoli)

Sfika

CAFE, BAR

11 🍷 Map p32, B4

It doesn't get much more local than this. Sfika, which translates to 'wasp', is a small neighbourhood cafe-restaurant-bar with an alternative/student vibe and occasional live music. (📞210 922 1341; Stratigou Kontouli 15, Makrygianni; 🕓9am-late; Ⓜ Akropoli)

Tiki Athens

BAR

12 🍷 Map p32, C3

Funky '50s decor, lots of varied music, an Asian-inspired menu and an alternative young crowd make this a

◯ Local Life

Ancient Promenade

The once-traffic-choked streets around Athens' historic centre were transformed into a spectacular 3km pedestrian promenade connecting the city's most significant ancient sites. In the evenings locals and tourists alike come out in force for an evening *volta* (walk) along the stunning cobblestone boulevard – one of Europe's longest pedestrian precincts – under the floodlit Acropolis.

The grand promenade starts at Dionysiou Areopagitou, opposite the Temple of Olympian Zeus, and continues along the southern foothills of the Acropolis, all the way to the Ancient Agora, branching off from Thisio to Keramikos and Gazi, and north along Adrianou to Monastiraki and Plaka.

fun place for a drink. (☏210 923 6908; www.tikiathens.com; Falirou 15, Makrygianni; ☉4.30pm-late; Ⓜ Akropoli)

Sports Club   BAR

13 ⓨ Map p32, C3

Americanos, Americanos, Americanos! You'll find a solid collection of them here at this bar run by the proprietors of Athens Backpackers. (Veikou 3a, Makrygianni; ☉7.30am-late; Ⓜ Akropoli)

Lamda Club   GAY

14 ⓨ Map p32, D3

Busy, three-level Lamda Club is not for the faint of heart. Look for the λ symbol on the sign. (☏210 942 4202; Lembesi 15, Makrygianni; Ⓜ Akropoli)

Shopping

El.Marneri Galerie   JEWELLERY, ARTS

15 🔒 Map p32, D3

Sample rotating exhibitions of local modern art and some of the best jewellery in the city. Handmade, unusual, and totally eye-catching. (☏210 861 9488; www.elenimarneri.com; Lembesi 5-7, Makrygianni; ☉10am-8pm Tue, Thu & Fri, to 6pm Wed & Sat; Ⓜ Akropoli)

Kanakis   JEWELLERY

16 🔒 Map p32, D3

A stunning range of contemporary jewellery from Cretan Spiros Kanakis, who often plays on ancient Greek motifs in his original gold designs; mostly handmade in his Iraklio workshop. (☏210 922 8297; Stratigou Makrygianni 17, Makrygianni; ☉11.30am-7pm Tue, Thu & Fri, to 6pm Wed & Sat; Ⓜ Akropoli)

Explore

Ancient Agora, Monastiraki & Psyrri

Monastiraki's central square (pictured, above) opens onto its jam-packed flea market, a warren of antique shops and great people-watching. To the south, the Ancient Agora was the city's original civic meeting place and remains a wonderful site to explore. Just north of Monastiraki lies Psyrri, where dilapidated facades belie the lively quarter where restaurants and bars coexist with warehouse conversions and workshops.

The Sights in a Day

☀ Start the day wandering the **Ancient Agora** (p40) and examining the priceless artefacts in its excellent museum housed in the Stoa of Attalos. If time permits, check out the elaborately carved **Tower of the Winds** (p48) at the **Roman Agora** (p48).

☀ Break for lunch along Adrianou at **Kuzina** (p51) or another of the plethora of cafes and restaurants, or find your way to **Café Avyssinia** (p51) for Acropolis views and old-world elegance. Then cruise the **Monastiraki flea market** (p45) and shop for souvenirs in its wild array of shops, such as **Olgianna Melissinos** (p53) with its handcrafted sandals and leather goods. Or swing into **Spiliopoulos** (p54) for discount designer duds and **Olgianna Melissinos** (p53) for handcrafted sandals and leather goods.

☽ Wrap up your day at **Magaze** (p53) or **Rooster** (p53) for pre-dinner cocktails, then choose between great local music with your dinner at **Akordeon** (p51) or savoury street fare at **Thanasis** (p52). As it nears midnight, make your way to **Booze Cooperativa** (p52), **Baba Au Rum** (p53), **Six DOGS** (p45) or other myriad bars to party the night away.

For a local's day exploring Monastiraki, see p44.

◉ Top Sights
Ancient Agora (p40)

○ Local Life
Exploring Monastiraki (p44)

♥ Best of Athens
Food
Cafe Avyssinia (p51)

Akordeon (p51)

Kostas (p45)

Thanasis (p52)

Shopping
Monastiraki Flea Market (p45)

Mompso (p45)

Martinos (p54)

Spiliopoulos (p54)

Olgianna Melissinos (p53)

Melissinos Art (p54)

Sabater Hermanos (p55)

Getting There

Ⓜ **Metro** Monastiraki station (blue and green lines) sits at the edge of the flea market, and the Ancient and Roman Agoras are a short walk south. Thisio station (green line) is just to the west of Monastiraki, and also offers easy access. Psyrri lies just to the north of both stations.

Top Sights
Ancient Agora

The heart of ancient Athens was the 6th-century-BC Agora, the lively focal point of administrative, commercial, political and social activity. Socrates expounded his philosophy here, and in AD 49 St Paul came here to win converts to Christianity. Devastated by the Persians in 480 BC, it was re-built and flourished through Pericles' time right up until AD 267, when it was destroyed by the Herulians. The Turks built a residential quarter here, but archaeologists demolished it after Independence and later excavated to classical and, in parts, neolithic levels.

👁 Map p46, D4

📞 210 321 0185

http://odysseus.culture.gr

Adrianou

adult/child €4/free, with Acropolis pass free

🕗 8am-8pm daily, reduced hours in low season

Ⓜ Monastiraki

Temple of Hephaestus

Don't Miss

Stoa of Attalos

A *stoa* is a covered walkway or portico, and the grand Stoa of Attalos served as the first-ever shopping arcade. Built by King Attalos II of Pergamum (159–138 BC), this majestic two-storey *stoa* has 45 Doric columns on the ground floor and Ionic columns on the upper gallery. The *stoa* was reconstructed between 1953 and 1956 by the American School of Archaeology, and originally the facade was painted red and blue.

Agora Museum

The excellent Agora Museum is housed inside the Stoa of Attalos. It is a great place to start, as it gives context to the site and has a model of the Agora to help get an overview. The museum displays a fine collection of finds from the site, with a special emphasis on early Athenian democracy. Artefacts range from early voting ballots and an ancient clock to early coins and terracotta figurines. Some of the oldest finds date from 4000 BC.

Ancient Statues

Around the *stoa*'s balconies you will find magnificent marble and bronze statues of the Greek gods. The sculptures date from 5th century BC to the 3rd century AD. Look for the two Nike statues, one in bronze, with inlaid eyes, as well as a winged interpretation in marble.

Temple of Hephaestus

The best-preserved Doric temple in Greece, this gem on the western edge of the Agora was dedicated to Hephaestus, god of the forge, and was surrounded by foundries and metalwork shops. Built in 449 BC by Iktinos, one of the architects of the Parthenon, it has 34 columns and a frieze on the eastern side depicting nine of the Twelve Labours of Hercules. In AD 1300 it was converted into the Church of Agios Georgios.

☑ Top Tips

▶ There are a couple of entrances, but the most convenient is the northern entrance on Adrianou, easily accessible from the metro and Monastiraki's flea market.

▶ Save time for the museum – it is packed with superb ancient artefacts.

▶ Have a photo op at the Temple of Hephaestus – it's one of the best-preserved temples in Greece and you can get quite close to it.

▶ Hours change. Call ahead to check.

✕ Take a Break

The site of the Agora today is a lush, refreshing respite from congested city streets. To sit a spell, exit the northern entrance onto Adrianou, where you can enjoy a coffee or a meal at Kuzina (p51) or Dioskouri (p52).

Stoa Foundations

To the northeast of the Temple of Hephaestus lie the foundations of the Stoa of Zeus Eleutherios, one of the places where Socrates expounded his philosophy. Further north are the foundations of the Stoa of Basileios and the Stoa Poikile. Stoa Poikile means 'Painted Stoa'; it was so-called because of its murals, which were rendered by the leading artists of the day and depicted mythological and historical battles.

Council House & Tholos

Though the Turks built a residential quarter throughout the Agora, it was demolished by archaeologists after Independence and later excavated to

what you see today. To the southeast of the Temple of Hephaestus they found the New Bouleuterion (Council House), where the Senate (originally created by Solon) met, while the heads of government met to the south at the circular Tholos.

Church of the Holy Apostles

This charming little Byzantine church, near the southern entrance, was built in the early 10th century to commemorate St Paul's teaching in the Agora. During the period of Ottoman rule, it underwent many changes, but between 1954 and 1957 it was stripped of its 19th-century additions and restored to its original form. It contains several fine Byzantine frescoes, which were transferred from a demolished church.

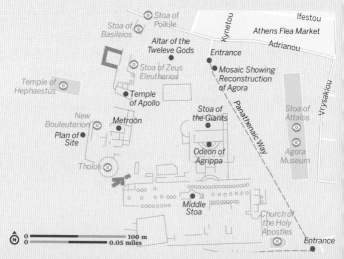

Understand

The Panathenaic Festival

The largest event in ancient Athens was the Panathenaic Procession, the climax of the Panathenaia Festival held to venerate the goddess Athena, the patron of the city. There were actually two types of festival. The more sedate Lesser Panathenaic Festival took place annually on Athena's birthday, approximately in July, while the Great Panathenaic Festival was held on every fourth anniversary of her birth.

The Great Panathenaic Festival began with dancing, followed by athletic, dramatic, poetic and musical contests. Among the athletic events, many held in the **Panathenaic Stadium** (p94) from the 4th century, were wrestling, pancratium (an ancient sport blending boxing and wrestling), pentathlon, footraces and chariot races. Winners were usually presented with amphorae (vase-shaped ceramic vessels) containing oil from the sacred olive trees of Athens, and victors might have received up to 140 of them.

The Panathenaic Procession

On the final day of the festival, the Panathenaic Procession began at the Dipylon Gate at Keramikos. Keramikos was also the spot where many of the animals sacrificed to Athena were feasted on at its Pompeion. The procession was led by men carrying more sacrificial animals, followed by maidens carrying *rhytons* (horn-shaped drinking vessels) and musicians playing a fanfare for the girls of noble birth who held aloft the sacred *peplos* (a glorious saffron-coloured shawl). During the preceding year, this select group of young women wove the *peplos* for the festival – a great honour.

The procession followed the Panathenaic Way, which cuts across the Ancient Agora and the middle of the Acropolis, leading to the Erechtheion. Not everyone was allowed to enter the Acropolis, but the favoured few ultimately placed the *peplos* on the statue of Athena Polias in the Erechtheion during the festival's grand finale.

Colourful scenes of the procession are depicted in the 160m-long Parthenon frieze in the Acropolis Museum (p30), and the British Museum.

Local Life
Exploring Monastiraki

Emerging at Monastiraki station you are confronted with all of Athens' character – the Acropolis looming above, souvlaki aromas wafting from Mitropoleos and the bustling flea market filling tiny pedestrian-only lanes. Wander the warren of shops and ateliers, dine at popular cafes and restaurants or simply people-watch in Plateia Monastirakiou (Monastiraki Sq).

❶ Plateia Avyssinias
Start your day with coffee at **Loukoumi** (www.loukoumibar.gr; Plateia Avyssinias 3, Monastiraki; ⏱11am-2am; Ⓜ Monastiraki), one flight above quaint Plateia Avyssinias. This artsy cafe filled with unique tables and chairs evokes the furniture market below. From there, explore the antique vendors around the *plateia*.

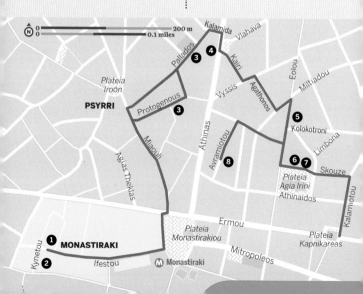

2 Monastiraki Flea Market

Join the hordes of locals combing Athens' **flea market** (btwn Adrianou, Ifestou & Ermou, Monastiraki; ☺daily; MMonastiraki). This eclectic sprawl is *the* place to stumble on anything from military boots, old books and antiques to furniture and collectables. It's in its element on Sundays, when vendors line up along Adrianou, cafes reach bursting and the area rings with a festive atmosphere.

3 Pallados & Protogenous Streets

Wander the length of these eclectic shopping streets, from cool basement shop **Color Skates** (✆210 331 7119; www.colorskates.com; Protogenous 5, Psyrri; ☺11am-5pm Mon, Wed & Sat, to 9pm Tue, Thu & Fri, noon-6pm Sun; MMonastiraki) with all manner of skate gear to **AD Gallery** (✆210 322 8785; www.adgallery.gr; Pallados 3, Psyrri; ☺noon-9pm Tue-Fri, to 4pm Sat, closed Aug; MMonastiraki), home to cutting-edge contemporary Greek artists. At the northeast end of Pallados, vendors hawk baskets and an industrial rope store offers cords in every material and colour.

4 Equestrian Crafts

Mompso (✆210 323 0670; www.mompso. com; Athinas 33, Psyrri; ☺10am-6pm Mon-Sat; MMonastiraki) is not to be missed. Find all manner of equestrian supplies and traditional accessories for donkeys (beaded headdresses), shepherds (bronze bells) and country folk (walking sticks) – they make unique souvenirs and gifts.

5 Mama Roux for Lunch

Mama Roux (✆213 004 8382; Eolou 48-50, Monastiraki; mains €5-13; ☺9am-midnight Tue-Sat, to 6pm Mon, noon-5pm Sun; 🛜; MMonastiraki), one of downtown's hot cheap-eats restaurants, fills up with locals digging into a fresh, delicious mix of food: from real burritos and Cajun specials to whopping American-style burgers. Reserve ahead.

6 Top Souvlaki

Stroll down to pretty Plateia Agia Irini to **Kostas** (✆210 323 2971; Plateia Agia Irini 2, Monastiraki; souvlaki €2; ☺9am-5pm; MMonastiraki). At this tiny hole-in-the-wall, young Kosta continues his grandfather's tradition, churning out tasty pork souvlakia with his signature spicy tomato sauce.

7 Afternoon Pick-Me-Up

Wander the textile shops on Kalamioutou, then circle back and check out **Tailor Made** (✆213 004 9645; www. tailormade.gr; Plateia Agia Irini 2, Monastiraki; ☺8am-2am; MMonastiraki), the super-popular microroastery with fab coffees, hand-pressed teas, homemade desserts and sandwiches. Cheerful Athenians spill out onto tables alongside the flower market. At night it's a happening cocktail and wine bar.

8 Hit the Clubs

Multiuse spaces morph from gallery to cafe to bar. **Six DOGS** (✆210 321 0510; www.sixdogs.gr; Avramiotou 6, Monastiraki; ☺10am-late; MMonastiraki) has a garden courtyard, while the bar jams at night with live theatre and art exhibitions.

A | B | C | D

1

Psaromilingou
Agion Asomaton
Dipylou
Tombazi
Kriezi
Sarri
Krahaou
Palamidou Rea
Agion Anargyron
🔒 34
15 ❌
Taki
32
PSYRR
Esopou
Mikon

2

Melidoni
Tournavitou
Sarri
Lepeniotou
Leokoriou
Ivis
Ogygou
Navarhou Apostoli
Aviton
Hristokopidou
Karais
Plateia Agion Asomaton
16 ❌
12
Ermou

3

Eptahalkou
Amfiktyonos
Agion Asomaton
Plateia Thisiou
Thisio Ⓜ
Thisiou
Astingos
🎫 26
18 ❌
11 ❌
Plate Avyssin
🔒 33
Ifest
Agiou Filippou
Kynetou
13 ❌
Adrianou
Poulopoulou

4

Vasilis
THISIO
Apostolou Pavlou
Iraklidon
Nileos
Akamandos
Ancient Agora 🔆

5

Ⓝ 0 _____ 200 m
0 _____ 0.1 miles

A.antonopoulou.art

9 Agiou
Dimitriou →

Museum
of Greek
Gastronomy **6**

20

Plateia
Iroón

Pallados

25 Protogenous

Kodrika

Vyssis

Polyklitou

Hrysospiliotissis

PraxiteIou

Ag Markou

Nikiou

Agathonos

Eolou

Leoharous

Agias Theklas

Miaouli

Themidos

Athinas

Avramiotou

Voreou

Karori

Eolou

Limbona

Kolokotroni

21

Klitiou

22

Romvis

Perikleous

Agias Irinis

24

Plateia
Agia Irini

Skouze

23

Athinaidos

14

Kalamiotou

Kevitos

28

Ermou

Plateia
Monastirakiou

29

Church of **4**
Kapnikarea

Plateia
Kapnikareas

LO
7

ormanou

Monastiraki
MONASTIRAKI

19

Plateia
Dimopratiriou

31

30

Museum **7**
of Traditional
Greek Ceramics

Kapnikareas

Vlahou Ang

Mitropoleos

Plateia
Mitropoleos **3**

Athens
Cathedral

Adrianou

Areos

Pandrosou

Hadrian's
Library **5**

Kladou

Dexippou

Kalogrioni

Plateia Arhaia
Agoras

Mnisikleous

PLAKA

Agias Filotheis

Peikilis

Epaminonda

Eolou

Adrianou

Diogenous

Taxiarhon

Roman **1**
Agora

2

Tower
of the
Winds

Markou Aureliou

Bath House
of the
Winds **8**

Kyrristou

Dioskouron

Panos

Thrasyvoulou

Lyssiou

Flessa

Mitroou

Nisiou

Sights

Roman Agora   HISTORIC SITE

1 ◉ Map p46, F5

The city's civic centre under Roman rule was moved to this partly excavated site, where you can see the foundations of several structures, including a 1st-century, 68-seat public latrine to the right of the entry, and a propylon (entrance) at the southeastern corner. The well-preserved Gate of Athena Archegetis, flanked by four Doric columns, was erected in the 1st century AD and financed by Julius Caesar. The Fethiye Djami mosque on the northern side of the Agora is one of the city's few surviving reminders of Ottoman times. Pre-dating the Agora is the fascinating Tower of the Winds. (☎ 210 324 5220; cnr Pelopida & Eolou, Monastiraki; adult/child €2/1, with Acropolis pass free; ⏰ 8am-3pm; Ⓜ Monastiraki)

Tower of the Winds   MONUMENT

2 ◉ Map p46, F5

The well-preserved Tower of the Winds was built in the 1st century BC by a Syrian astronomer named Andronicus. The octagonal monument of Pentelic marble is an ingenious construction that functioned as a sundial, weathervane, water clock and compass. Each side represents a point of the compass, and has a relief of a figure floating through the air, which depicts the wind associated with that particular point. Beneath each of the reliefs are the faint markings of sundials. (Roman Agora; Ⓜ Monastiraki)

Athens Cathedral   CHURCH

3 ◉ Map p46, H4

The ornate 1862 Athens Cathedral on Plateia Mitropoleos (Mitropoleos Sq) is the seat of the archbishop of the Greek Orthodox Church of Athens. However, far more significant, both historically and architecturally, is the small, 12th-century, cruciform-style marble church next to the cathedral, known as the **Little Metropolis**, officially dedicated to two saints as the Church of Panagia Gorgeopikoos (Virgin Swift to Hear) and Agios Eleftherios. It was built on the ruins of an ancient temple using reliefs and pieces of ancient and early-Christian monuments. (☎ 210 322 1308; Plateia Mitropoleos, Monastiraki; ⏰ 7am-7pm, Mass Sun 6.30am; Ⓜ Monastiraki)

Church of Kapnikarea   CHURCH

4 ◉ Map p46, G3

This small 11th-century structure stands smack in the middle of the Ermou shopping strip. It was saved from the bulldozers and restored by Athens University. Its dome is supported by four large Roman columns. (Ermou, Monastiraki; ⏰ 8am-2pm Tue, Thu & Fri; Ⓜ Monastiraki, Syntagma)

Understand

Roman Rule

-- -- -- -- -- -- -- -- -- -- -- -- -- -- -- -- --

The First Incursions

During the 4th century BC, while Alexander the Great of Macedon (geographically the modern prefecture of Macedonia) was ruling the Greek city-states and forging his vast empire through Persia and into the east, the Romans were expanding their empire to the west, and began making inroads into Greece. After Alexander's death in 323 BC, Macedonia lost control of the southern Greek city-states, which banded together into the Aetolian League, centred on Delphi, and the Achaean League, based in the Peloponnese. Athens and Sparta joined neither.

Roman Victories

After several inconclusive clashes, the Romans finally defeated Macedon in 168 BC at the Battle of Pydna. The Achaean League was defeated in 146 BC and the Roman consul Mummius made an example of the rebellious Corinthians by destroying their city.

In 86 BC Athens joined an ill-fated rebellion against the Romans in Asia Minor staged by the king of the Black Sea region, Mithridates VI. In retribution, the fierce Roman statesman Sulla invaded Athens, destroyed the city walls and carted off many of its finest statues to Rome. At this point, Greece became the Graeco-Roman province of Achaea. Although officially under the auspices of Rome, several major Greek cities were given the freedom to self-govern to some extent.

The Pax Romana

Because the Romans revered Greek culture, Athens retained its status as a centre of learning. The city received a pardon for its rebellion from Julius Caesar, and for the next 300 years it experienced an unprecedented period of peace – the Pax Romana – which lasted until the middle of the 3rd century AD. During this time it became the seat of learning for the Romans as well, attracting the sons of wealthy Romans. During the Pax Romana, a succession of Roman emperors, namely Augustus, Nero and particularly Hadrian, graced Athens with many grand buildings, including the Roman Agora and Hadrian's library (p50) and territorial **arch** (cnr Leoforos Vasilissis Olgas & Leoforos Vasilissis Amalias, Syntagma; admission free; MAkropoli, Syntagma).

Hadrian's Library   RUIN

5 ◉ Map p46, F4

To the north of the Roman Agora is
this vast 2nd-century-AD library, the
largest structure erected by Hadrian.
It included a cloistered courtyard
bordered by 100 columns, and a pool in
the centre. As well as books, the building housed music and lecture rooms
and a theatre. (☑ 210 324 9350; Areos 3,
Monastiraki; adult/child €2/free, with Acropolis
pass free; ⊙8am-3pm, reduced hours in low
season; Ⓜ Monastiraki)

Museum of Greek
Gastronomy   MUSEUM

6 ◉ Map p46, E1

This new museum and culinary centre
creates specialised displays highlight-
ing one aspect of Greece's rich culinary
history (say, organic monastery food,
or the traditions of Macedonia). Its

cafe-restaurant then serves up creative
dishes (€7 to €15) tied to the exhibition, and the shop sells goods from
each theme, whether it's Macedonian
honey or monastery-made jam. It also
has occasional cooking classes, film
screenings and parties. (☑ 210 321 1311;
www.gastronomymuseum.gr; Agiou Dimitriou
13, Psyrri; admission free; ⊙11am-6pm Tue, to
midnight Wed-Sun, restaurant 5pm-midnight
Wed-Sun; Ⓜ Monastiraki, Thisio)

Museum of Traditional
Greek Ceramics   MUSEUM

7 ◉ Map p46, F3

The Mosque of Tzistarakis (built in
1759) is one of few surviving examples
of a *tzami* (mosque) in Athens. It
houses the annexe of the Museum of
Greek Folk Art and features pottery
and hand-painted ceramics from the
early 20th century. At the time of
writing it was temporarily closed.
(☑ 210 324 2066; www.melt.gr; Areos 1,
Monastiraki; Ⓜ Monastiraki)

Bath House of
the Winds   MUSEUM

8 ◉ Map p46, G5

This beautifully refurbished 17th-
century *hammam* (Turkish bath) is
the only surviving public bathhouse in
Athens and one of the few remnants
of Ottoman times. A helpful free audio
tour takes you back to its glory days.
(☑ 210 324 4340; www.melt.gr; Kyrristou 8,
Monastiraki; adult/child €2/free, Sun Nov-Mar
free; ⊙8am-3pm Wed-Mon; Ⓜ Monastiraki)

◯ Local Life
Mezedhes & Ouzo

Join young Athenians at **Kallipateira** (☑ 210 321 4152; www.kallipateira.
gr; Astingos 8, Monastirkai; dishes €4-10;
⊙lunch & dinner; Ⓜ Monastiraki) as
they gather for long sessions over
carafes of ouzo, snacking on one
of the *pikilies* (mixed mezedhes).
Thursday to Sunday acoustic
rembetika (Greek blues) and Cretan
live music rocks out this neoclassic
building overlooking an archaeological dig.

A.antonopoulou.art GALLERY

9 ◉ Map p46, E1

One of the original galleries to open in Psyrri's warehouses, this impressive art space hosts a range of exhibitions of contemporary and international art, including installations, video art and photography by emerging Greek artists. (☎210 321 4994; www.aaart.gr; 4th fl, Aristofanous 20, Psyrri; ⊙10am-8pm Tue-Fri; ⓜMonastiraki)

Taf GALLERY

10 ◉ Map p46, E3

The central courtyard cafe at Taf, surrounded by crumbling 1870s brick buildings, fills with an eclectic young crowd. The rest functions as an art, music and theatre space where performances and screenings are often free. (The Art Foundation; ☎210 323 8757; www.theartfoundation. gr; Normanou 5, Monastiraki; ⊙noon-9pm Mon-Sat, to 7pm Sun; ⓜMonastiraki)

Eating

Café Avyssinia MEZEDHES €€

11 ✕ Map p46, D3

Hidden away on colourful Plateia Avyssinias, in the middle of the flea market, this bohemian *mezedhopoleio* (restaurant specialising in mezedhes) gets top marks for atmosphere, food and friendly service. It specialises in regional Greek cuisine, from warm fava to eggplants baked with tomato and cheese, and has a great selection of ouzo, *raki* (Cretan

firewater) and *tsipouro* (a distilled spirit similar to ouzo but usually stronger). (☎210 321 7047; Kynetou 7, Monastiraki; mains €10-16; ⊙11am-1am Tue-Sat, to 7pm Sun; ⓜMonastiraki)

Akordeon MEZEDHES €

12 ✕ Map p46, D2

Slide into this charming butter yellow house across from a church in a quiet Psyrri side street for a warm welcome by musician-chefs Pepi and Achilleas (and their spouses), who run this excellent new entry on the local music and mezedhes scene. They'll help you order authentic Greek fare, then (at night and on weekends) surround you with their soulful songs. (☎210 325 3703; Hristokopidou 7, Psyrri; dishes €5-12; ⊙lunch & dinner; ⓜMonastiraki, Thisio)

Kuzina MODERN GREEK €€

13 ✕ Map p46, C3

Light streams through plate-glass windows, warming the crowded tables in winter. Or eat outside on pedestrianised, people-watching Adrianou in summer. Expect inventive Greek fusion, such as Cretan pappardelle or chicken with figs and sesame. (☎210 324 0133; www.kuzina.gr; Adrianou 9, Monastiraki; mains €12-25; ⊙11am-late; ⓜThisio)

Melilotos GREEK €

14 ✕ Map p46, H2

Great, affordable Greek food with a dash of sophistication and a dram of wine makes a fun start to a night out in the area's bar quarter. Specials rotate daily. (📞210 322 2458; www. melilotos.gr; Kalamiotou 19, Monastiraki; mains €6-10; ⏰noon-1am Tue-Sat, 2-10pm Sun; Ⓜ Monastiraki)

Nikitas   TAVERNA €

15 🍴 Map p46, D1

Locals swear by this tried-and-true taverna that has been serving reasonably priced, refreshingly simple and tasty traditional food since well before Psyrri became trendy. It's the only place busy on weekdays. (📞210 325 2591; Agion Anargyron 19, Psyrri; mains €6-8; ⏰noon-6pm; Ⓜ Monastiraki)

Ivis   MEZEDHES €

16 🍴 Map p46, C2

This cosy, corner *mezedhopoleio,* with its bright, arty decor, has a small but delicious range of simple, freshly cooked mezedhes. Ask for the daily specials as there's only a rough, hand-written menu in Greek. A good ouzo selection lights things up. (📞210 323 2554; Navarhou Apostoli 19, Psyrri; mezedhes €4-10; Ⓜ Thisio)

Dioskouri   MEZEDHES €

17 🍴 Map p46, E3

A landmark cafe sitting virtually over the railway line. Its tables sit under a huge plane tree and give it a traditional village feel. It's popular with students for mezedhes and ouzo. (📞210 325 3333; Adrianou 37, Monastiraki; mezedhes €3-8; ⏰8.30am-1am; Ⓜ Monastiraki)

Ouzou Melathron   MEZEDHES €

18 🍴 Map p46, D3

The famous *ouzerie* chain from Thessaloniki has been a hit since it opened right in the middle of the Monastiraki marketplace. It's a buzzing, unpretentious spot serving tasty mezedhes from a whimsical menu. (📞210 324 0716; Agiou Filipou 10, cnr Astingos, Monastiraki; mezedhes €5-7; ⏰noon-late; Ⓜ Monastiraki)

Thanasis   SOUVLAKI €

19 🍴 Map p46, F3

In the heart of Athens' souvlaki hub, at the end of Mitropoleos, Thanasis is known for its kebabs on pitta with grilled tomato and onions. (📞210 324 4705; Mitropoleos 69, Monastiraki; gyros €2.50; ⏰8.30am-2.30am; Ⓜ Monastiraki)

Taverna tou Psyrri   TAVERNA €

20 🍴 Map p46, E1

This cheerful taverna just off Plateia Iroön turns out decent, no-frills, traditional food. (📞210 321 4923; Eshylou 12, Psyrri; mains €6-9; ⏰lunch & dinner, closed 2 weeks Aug; Ⓜ Monastiraki)

Drinking

Booze Cooperativa   CAFE, BAR

21 🍷 Map p46, H2

By day, this laid-back, arty hang-out is full of young Athenians playing chess and backgammon and working on their Macs; later it transforms into a

Hot Grill

Telis (☎210 324 2775; Evripidou 86, Psyrri; pork chops €7; ⏰8am-2am Mon-Sat; Ⓜ Thisio) has been slaving over the flame grill at his eponymous fluoro-lit, bare-walled, paper-tablecloth *psistaria* (taverna that specialises in chargrilled or spit-roasted meat) cooking his famous pork chops, since 1978. There's nothing else on the menu – just meat, chips and Greek salad, washed down with rough house wine or beer.

happening bar that rocks till late. The basement hosts art exhibitions and there's a theatre upstairs. (☎211 405 3733; www.boozecooperativa.com; Kolokotroni 57, Monastiraki; ⏰11am-late; Ⓜ Monastiraki)

Baba Au Rum

COCKTAIL BAR

22 🍸 Map p46, H2

Fab cocktail mixologists concoct the tipples of your dreams. (☎211 710 9140; www.babaaurum.com; Klitiou 6, Monastiraki; ⏰5pm-3am Mon-Thu, noon-4am Fri & Sat, 1pm-2am Sun; Ⓜ Syntagma, Monastiraki)

Rooster

CAFE

23 🍸 Map p46, G2

This wonderfully packed gay cafe on lively Plateia Agia Irini is straight friendly too, and so fills with chatting locals. (www.roostercafe.gr; Plateia Agia Irini 4, Monastiraki; ⏰9am-3am; Ⓜ Monastiraki)

Magaze

CAFE

24 🍸 Map p46, G2

Gay-friendly Magaze has Acropolis views from footpath tables. (☎210 324 3740; Eolou 33, Monastiraki; ⏰noon-late; Ⓜ Monastiraki)

Tranzistor

BAR

25 🍸 Map p46, E2

Sidle up to the backlit bar or relax at tables outside at this teeny, cool spot. (☎210 322 8658; Protogenous 10, Psyrri; ⏰9am-midnight; Ⓜ Monastiraki)

James Joyce

PUB

26 🍸 Map p46, C3

The Guinness is free-flowing at this Irish pub, with decent food (mains €9 to €12), live music and loads of travellers and expats. (☎210 323 5055; www.jjoyceirishpubathens.com; Astingos 12, Monastiraki; ⏰10am-1am Sun-Thu, to 3am Fri & Sat; Ⓜ Monastiraki)

Shopping

Olgianna Melissinos

SHOES, ACCESSORIES

27 🔒 Map p46, E3

Olgianna Melissinos designs and crafts a wide range of excellent leather goods, from sandals to backpacks. Her father, Stavros, was a famous poet/sandal-maker whose customers included the Beatles, Sophia Loren and Jackie Onassis. She can make things to order. (📞210 331 1925; www.melissinos-sandals.gr; Normanou 7, Monastiraki; ⏱10am-6pm Mon, Wed, Sat & Sun, to 8pm Tue, Thu & Fri; Ⓜ Monastiraki)

Melissinos Art   SHOES

28 🔒 Map p46, E3

Pantelis Melissinos continues the sandal-making tradition of his famous poet/sandal-maker father Stavros. (📞210 321 9247; www.melissinos-art.com; Agias Theklas 2, Psyrri; ⏱10am-8pm, to 6pm winter; Ⓜ Monastiraki)

Spiliopoulos   SHOES, ACCESSORIES

29 🔒 Map p46, G3

Chaos reigns but you may find a bargain among the overcrowded racks of imported designer seconds and old-season shoes and bags. It also stocks leather jackets. There's a branch on Adrianou. (📞210 322 7590; Ermou 63, Monastiraki; ⏱10am-4.30pm Mon, Wed & Sat, to 8.30pm Tue, Thu & Fri; Ⓜ Monastiraki)

Centre of Hellenic Tradition   HANDICRAFTS

30 🔒 Map p46, F3

Traditional ceramics, sculpture and handicrafts from all parts of Greece. (📞210 321 3023; www.kelp.gr; Pandrosou 36, Monastiraki; ⏱9am-8pm Apr-Nov, to 6pm Oct-Mar; Ⓜ Monastiraki)

Martinos   ANTIQUES

31 🔒 Map p46, F3

This Monastiraki landmark opened in 1890 and has an excellent selection of Greek and European antiques and collectables, including painted dowry chests, icons, coins, glassware, porcelain and furniture. (📞210 321 2414; www.martinosart.gr; Pandrosou 50, Monastiraki; ⏱10am-3pm Mon, Wed & Sat, 10am-6pm Tue, Thu & Fri, closed Aug; Ⓜ Monastiraki)

Kartousa   JEWELLERY, HOMEWARES

32 🔒 Map p46, D2

Ecelctic handmade jewellery and homewares brighten this tiny store-

---

☑ Top Tip

Shoppers' Paradise

Shoppers should budget extra time to wander Monastiraki and Psyrri's warren of streets: from boutiques to districts entirely given over to a particular product (textiles, electronics, ribbons, religious paraphernalia etc), you could lost among all the options. Also bring a blank camera memory card – you'll find loads of cool streetside photo ops along the way.

Diners, Ouzou Melathron (p52)

front. (☏ 210 324 7525; Taki 9, Psyrri;
⏱ 11am-8pm Tue-Sat, from noon
Sun; Ⓜ Monastiraki)

John Samuelin   MUSIC

33 🔒 Map p46, D3

This central spot is jam-packed with
Greek and other musical instruments.
(☏ 210 321 2433; www.musicshop.gr; Ifestou
36, Monastiraki; ⏱ 9am-7pm; Ⓜ Monastiraki)

Sabater Hermanos   SOAP

34 🔒 Map p46, D1

This tiny, bright and cheery shop
is packed with colourful all-natural
soaps and bath crystals. (☏ 210 331
6824; Agion Anargyron 31, Psyrri; ⏱ 11am-
6pm, closed Aug; Ⓜ Thisio)

Local Life
Wandering the Central Market

Getting There

M From Monastiraki station (blue and green lines) walk up Athinas. From Omonia (red and green lines) walk down (south) Athinas. Panepistimio (red line) is three blocks east.

The streets around the colourful and bustling Athens Central Market (also referred to as the Varvakios Agora) are a sensory delight. Jam-packed with people shopping at the market – the highlight of the district – and at nearby spice and provisions shops, it also harbours some of *the* most classic local eating experiences, the city's best *rembetika* (Greek blues) joint, and cutting-edge art galleries.

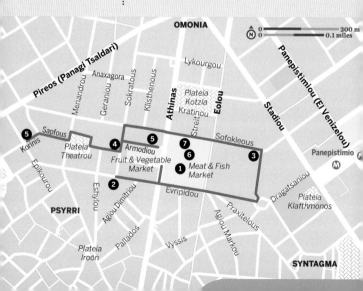

❶ Athens Central Market

This hectic, colourful **market** (Varvakios Agora; Athinas, btwn Sofokleous & Evripidou; ⏱7am-3pm Mon-Sat) is an explosion for the senses and a must for gastronomes, with an amazing range of olives, spices, cheeses and deli treats. Filling the historic building on the eastern side, the meat and fish market, with its hanging carcasses illuminated by swinging light bulbs, is a surreal highlight. The fruit and vegetable market is across the road.

❷ Spice Shops, Miran & More

Along the streets around the market, burlap bags overflow with chillies, dried rosebuds and candied ginger. Wander the shops enjoying the aromas emanating from within. Try **Bahar** (☎210 321 7225; www.bahar.gr; Evripidou 31, Omonia; ⏱7am-3pm Mon-Thu & Sat, to 6pm Fri) for a plethora of spices. **Miran** (☎210 321 7187; www.miran.gr; Evripidou 45, Psyrri) is the local favourite for prepared meats from sausage to prosciutto.

❸ Greek Regional Specialties

If you'd like a more structured shopping experience, head to **To Pantopoleion** (☎210 323 4612; www.atenco.gr; Sofokleous 1, Omonia; ⏱8am-7pm), which sells traditional food products from all over Greece. Find everything from Santorini capers to Cretan rusks, jars of goodies for edible souvenirs, and Greek wines and spirits.

❹ Quirky Taverna

There's no signage at **Diporto Agoras** (☎210 321 1463; cnr Theatrou & Sokratous; plates €5-6; ⏱7am-7pm Mon-Sat, closed 1-20 Aug), one of the dining gems of Athens. Double doors lead to a rustic cellar, where there's also no menu. The speciality is *revythia* (chickpeas), followed by grilled fish and washed down with wine from giant barrels. Often-erratic service is part of the appeal.

❺ Hot Contemporary Art

After lunch, hit two of Athens' most innovative modern-art galleries, which promote emerging local and visiting artists: **Qbox Gallery** (☎211 119 9991; www. qbox.gr; Armodiou 10, Monastiraki; ⏱noon-6pm Tue-Fri, to 4pm Sat) and **Andreas Melas & Helena Papadopoulos Gallery** (☎210 325 1881; www.melaspapadopoulos.com; Epikourou 26, cnr Korinis, Psyrri; ⏱noon-6pm Tue-Fri, to 4pm Sat).

❻ Late-Night Dinner

The meat market might sound like a strange place for a meal, but its meat tavernas are an Athenian institution, turning out huge quantities of tasty, traditional fare for everyone from market workers to late-night partiers.

❼ Rembetika

The legendary *rembetika* club **Stoa Athanaton** (☎210 321 4362; Sofokleous 19, Central Market, Omonia; ⏱3-6pm & midnight-6am Mon-Sat, closed Jun-Sep) occupies a hall above the central meat market. It remains *the* place to hear classic *rembetika* and *laïka* (urban popular music) from a respected band of musicians. Access is by a lift in the arcade.

Explore

Greek Parliament, Syntagma & Plaka

Syntagma is the heart of modern Athens, with Plateia Syntagmatos (Syntagma Sq) its historic meeting point, political centre and transport hub. The National Gardens offer welcome respite from the hustle, or it's a short walk to Plaka, which has undeniable charm. Plaka's narrow, paved streets pass by ancient sites, restored and crumblingneoclassical mansions, fascinating small museums, Byzantine churches and ambient tavernas.

The Sights in a Day

Start your day by exploring Athens' main shopping districts in Plaka and Syntagma. From creative jewellery like that at **Apriati** (p71), to handicrafts at **Aidini** (p71) or natural beauty supplies at **Korres** (p71), there's so much to see your head will be spinning. Break for lunch at a simple taverna like **Paradosiako** (p68), or eat organic at **Pure Bliss** (p67).

Visit the vast array of museums of Greek culture, such as **Kanellopoulos Museum** (p64) or the **Greek Folk Art Museum** (p66), or watch the **Changing of the Guard** (pictured, left; p64) and then hide from the heat in the verdant **National Gardens** (p64).

Dine at **Tzitzikas & Mermingas** (p67) or **2 Mazi** (p67) then go bar-hopping around Syntagma at places such as **Seven Jokers** (p68), **Galaxy Bar** (p69) and **Clumsies** (p68). Or for a more sedate evening, catch a flick at **Cine Paris** (p70), Plaka's outdoor cinema.

For a local's day shopping around Plaka, see p60.

Local Life

Shopping Around Plaka (p60)

Best of Athens

Museums

Kanellopoulos Museum (p64)

Greek Folk Art Museum (p66)

Jewish Museum (p64)

Food

2 Mazi (p67)

Tzitzikas & Mermingas (p67)

Kalnterimi (p67)

Avocado (p61)

Paradosiako (p68)

Bars

Clumsies (p68)

Seven Jokers (p68)

Brettos (p69)

Gin Joint (p61)

Getting There

M Metro Syntagma station (blue and red lines) sits at the heart of the city. You'll emerge at Plateia Syntagmatos, a short walk from Plaka. Plaka is easily reached from the Monastiraki station (blue and green lines) to the north, and the Akropoli station (red line) to the southwest.

Local Life
Shopping Around Plaka

Plaka's lower reaches are jammed with small museums, a slew of tavernas, and kitsch souvenir stores, especially on main streets like Kydathineon and Adrianou. Move away from the tourist strip for a glimpse of old Athens – virtually car free – in narrow lanes winding up the northeastern side of the Acropolis hill, and in the maze of the Anafiotika quarter. A jaunt north to the Syntagma area will bring you to one of Athens' hippest bar precincts.

❶ Breakfast Homage to Melina
Low-key **Melina** (Lyssiou 22, Plaka; ⏰9am-midnight; Ⓜ Akropoli, Monastiraki) is an ode to the late, great Mercouri. Decorated with memorabilia and photographs celebrating Greece's legendary actress and politician, this cafe offers charm and intimacy out of the hectic centre.

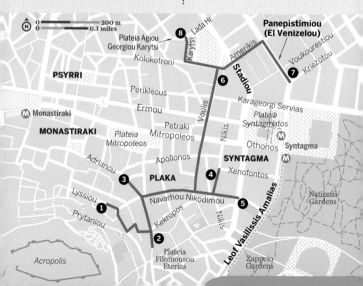

❷ Shopping Adrianou

Plaka is loaded with so-so vendors – instead, head to its best shops, the ones Athenians frequent. **Ioanna Kourbela** (☎210 322 4591; www.ioannakourbela.com; Adrianou 109, Plaka; ⏱10am-9pm Mon-Sat, from 11am Sun; Ⓜ Syntagma) designs classic, cool women's clothes: elegant cottons and silks in natural, warm tones.

❸ Creative Souvenirs

The impeccable small store **Forget Me Not** (☎210 325 3740; www.forgetmenot athens.gr; Adrianou 100, Plaka; ⏱10am-10pm May-Sep, to 8pm Oct-Apr; Ⓜ Syntagma, Monastiraki) stocks supercool design gear, from fashion to housewares by contemporary Greek designers. Souvenirs have never had it so good: from 'evil eye' coasters to Hermes rubber beach sandals.

❹ Snacks & Wine

Avocado (☎210 323 7878; www.avocadoathens.com; Nikis 30, Plaka; mains €6-12; ⏱11am-10pm Mon-Sat, to 7pm Sun; 🛜🖊; Ⓜ Syntagma) dishes up vegan, gluten-free and organic treats – a rarity in Greece. Enjoy everything from sandwiches to coconut curry on the tiny front patio. Juices and smoothies are made on the spot, or splash out on a bottle at **Wine Story** (☎210 323 9997; www.winestory.gr; Nikis 21, Plaka; ⏱9.30am-9.30pm Mon-Sat, 10am-2pm & 5-9pm Sun; Ⓜ Syntagma), across the street.

❺ Byzantine Church

Break from shopping and visit **Sotira Lykodimou** (Fillelinon, Plateia Rallou Manou, Plaka; Ⓜ Syntagma), built in 1031. It is the largest medieval structure (and only octagonal Byzantine church) in Athens, and has served as the Russian Orthodox Church since 1847.

❻ Chocolate Indulgence

For a sweet pick-me-up head to **Aristokratikon** (☎210 323 4373; www.aristo kratikon.com; Voulis 7, Syntagma; ⏱8am-9pm Mon-Fri, to 6pm Sat; Ⓜ Syntagma), where chocaholics will be thrilled by the dazzling array of handmade chocolates at this tiny store that's been around since 1928. Karageorgi Servias is also loaded with sweet and dried-nut shops.

❼ Mastiha Shop

While you're in the neighbourhood, swing over to **Mastiha Shop** (☎210 363 2750; www.mastihashop.com; Panepistimiou 6, Syntagma; ⏱9am-9pm; Ⓜ Syntagma), purveyor of all things mastic: the medicinal resin from rare mastic trees produced only on the island of Chios. The liqueur is divine when served chilled, but there are also skin products, essential oils and foodstuffs.

❽ Clubbing in Syntagma

After you've rested up and grabbed some nourishment for the night, head to the area around Plateia Karytsi and Kolokotroni for central Athens' best bar scene. One such bar is called **Gin Joint** (☎210 321 8646; Christou Lada 1, Syntagma; ⏱noon-2am; Ⓜ Syntagma) for a reason: sample 60 gins or other fancy cocktails, some with historical notes on their origin.

City of Athens Museum 7

17

12

20 Kolokot

23

19 Thiseos

13 Romvis

Klitiou

Plateia Agia Irini

Skouze

Athinaidos

Limbona

Perikleous

MONASTIRAKI

Ermou

Plateia Kapnikareas

Monastiraki Pandrosou

Mitropoleos

Evangelistrias

Fokionos

Petraki

9 Greek Folk Art Museum

Eolou

Dexippou

Plateia Mitropoleos

Ipatias

Patrou

Apollonos

Adrianou

Benizelou Paleologou

Agias Filotheis

Thoukididou

PLAKA

Ipi

Pelopida

8 Museum of Greek Popular Instruments

Areos

Mnisikleous

30

Kyrristou

Navarhou Nikodimou

26 Thrasyvoulou

Lyssiou

Flessa

Scholiou

Adrianou

Kekropos

Kanellopoulos Museum

Erehtheos

29

16

4 Theorias

Prytaniou

ANAFIOTIKA

Tripodon

14

28

PLAKA

Stratonos

Rangava

Kydathine

Plateia Filomousou Eterias

21

Iperid

Praxitelous

Pallados

Athinas

Vyssis

Miltiadou

Nikiou

Plate Karyt

Miaouli

Avramiotou

Karori

Thraki

E F G H

Panepistimiou (El Venizelou)

▲ 35

N 0 ──── 200 m
  0 ──── 0.1 miles

Akadimias

Pindarou

Solonos

Stadiou

Plateia
Kolokotroni
● 6

National
Historical
Museum
● 18

● 22

Amerikis

● 25

Voukourestiou

● 40

Kriezotou

● 36

Kanari

KOLONAKI

Merlin

Sekeri

● 38

32
●

Zalokosta

Voulis

Karageorgi Servias

Nikis

Vasileos Georgiou I

Leof Vasilissis Sofias

Ermou

33 ●

SYNTAGMA

Stadiou

● 11

Plateia
Syntagmatos
● 1

M

Syntagma

M

M Syntagma

2
● Parliament &
Changing of
the Guard

Othonos

9

Skoufou

31
●

Nikis

Filellinon

Xenofontos

3 National
● Gardens

4

● 34

Souri G

10 ●

Jewish
Museum
● 5

Plateia Rallou
Manou

Leof Vasilissis Amalias

eia
ros

Kydathineon

Tsatsou K

Dedalou

27 ✿

Zappeio
Gardens

1

2

3

4

5

For reviews see

⊙	Sights	p64
⊗	Eating	p67
⊜	Drinking	p68
✿	Entertainment	p70
⌂	Shopping	p71

Sights

Plateia Syntagmatos
SQUARE

1 ⊙ Map p62, F3

Athens' central square is named for the constitution granted, after uprisings, by King Otto on 3 September 1843. Today, the square serves as a major transport hub, the location of parliament (on the eastern, uphill side) and also, therefore, the epicentre of demonstrations and strikes. (Constitution Sq; Ⓜ Syntagma)

Parliament & Changing of the Guard
BUILDING

2 ⊙ Map p62, G3

In front of the parliament building on Plateia Syntagmatos, the traditionally costumed *evzones* (guards) of the Tomb of the Unknown Soldier change every hour on the hour. On Sunday at 11am, a whole platoon marches down Vasilissis Sofias to the tomb, accompanied by a band.

The presidential guards' uniform of short kilts and pom-pom shoes is based on the attire worn by the *klephts* (the mountain fighters of the War of Independence). (Plateia Syntagmatos; admission free; Ⓜ Syntagma)

National Gardens
GARDENS

3 ⊙ Map p62, H4

A delightful, shady refuge during summer, the National Gardens were formerly the royal gardens, designed by Queen Amalia. There's a large children's playground, a duck pond and a shady cafe. (cnr Leoforos Vasilissis Sofias & Leoforos Vasilissis Amalias, Syntagma; admission free; ⊙ 7am-dusk; Ⓜ Syntagma)

Kanellopoulos Museum
MUSEUM

4 ⊙ Map p62, A5

This excellent museum, in a 19th-century mansion on the northern slope of the Acropolis, houses the Kanellopoulos family's extensive collection, donated to the state in 1976. The collection includes jewellery, clay and stone vases and figurines, weapons, Byzantine icons, bronzes and objets d'art. (☎ 210 321 2313; http://odysseus.culture.gr; Theorias 12, cnr Panos, Plaka; admission €2; ⊙ 8am-3pm Tue-Sun, reduced hours in low season; Ⓜ Monastiraki)

Jewish Museum
MUSEUM

5 ⊙ Map p62, E4

This museum traces the history of the Jewish community in Greece – back to the 3rd century BC – through an impressive collection of documents and religious and folk art. It includes a small reconstruction of a synagogue. (☎ 210 322 5582; www.jewishmuseum.gr; Nikis 39, Plaka; adult/child €6/free; ⊙ 9am-2.30pm Mon-Fri, 10am-2pm Sun; Ⓜ Syntagma)

Understand
Greece's Political & Economic Situation
-- -- -- -- -- -- -- -- -- -- -- -- -- -- -- -- -- -- --

In December 2009 newly elected Prime Minister George Papandreou revealed to the world that Greece's debts had reached €300 billion (113% of GDP – nearly double the eurozone limit of 60%). Ratings agencies started downgrading Greek debt and the ultimate spiral of economic depression and possible default began. Greece's total debt soared, reaching 165.3% of GDP in 2011 and has not fallen much since then.

The Bailouts
Between 2010 and 2012, the troika (European Commission, European Central Bank and International Monetary Fund) approved two bailout loan packages totalling €240 billion (not all of which was disbursed) to prevent Greece from defaulting on its debt. The deals required the government to impose strict austerity measures (public spending and pension cuts, tax-evasion crack-down and tax increases) and to raise billions through the privatisation of state-controlled assets. And 2012 also saw a 'debt swap' or 'haircut' whereby debt to private lenders was reduced by half.

The country has fallen into a deeper depression: GDP shrunk by about 20% during five years. By 2013, unemployment had risen to 26.8%, with youth unemployment at a staggering 60%. By 2014 unemployment climbed to 28%. In early 2015 when the ECB cut off emergency aid (already totalling €130 billion), the banks closed briefly and capital controls were imposed, and remain in effect as of the time of writing.

The Human Costs
Throughout this saga tumultuous human, social and political repercussions have rocked Greece. These include mass protests and widespread strikes. Disillusionment with the long-ruling PASOK and New Democracy parties ultimately saw Alexis Tsipras of the leftist anti-austerity party Syriza get elected prime minister in January 2015. As Greece teeters on the brink of default, talks with the troika remain embattled as a third loan package and debt restructuring are being negotiated. The possibility remains that Greece could exit the eurozone.

The reality of lost jobs, capital controls, cut wages and pensions, un-payable taxes, and disappearing social services has been exacerbated by the uncertainty that accompanies each of these political and economic manoeuvres.

National Historical Museum

MUSEUM

6 ◉ Map p62, E1

Specialising in memorabilia from the War of Independence (1821–27), this museum houses Byron's helmet and sword, a series of paintings depicting events leading up to the war and a collection of photographs and royal portraits. The museum is housed in the old parliament building, on the steps of which Prime Minister Theodoros Deligiannis was assassinated in 1905. (☏210 323 7617; www.nhmuseum.gr; Stadiou 13, Syntagma; adult/child €3/ free, Sun free; ⏱9am-2pm Tue-Sun; Ⓜ Syntagma)

City of Athens Museum

MUSEUM

7 ◉ Map p62, D1

Housed in two interconnected historic buildings, including the palace where King Otto lived between 1830 and 1846, this museum contains an extensive collection of royal furniture, antiques, paintings and personal mementos, as well as a model of 1842 Athens and a massive painting showing Athens before the Venetian destruction in 1687. The 2nd-floor gallery hosts temporary exhibitions. (☏210 323 1397; www.athenscitymuseum.gr; Paparigopoulou 7, Syntagma; adult/child €3/ free; ⏱9am-4pm Mon & Wed-Fri, 10am-3pm Sat & Sun; Ⓜ Panepistimio)

Museum of Greek Popular Instruments

MUSEUM

8 ◉ Map p62, B4

More than 1200 folk instruments dating from the 18th century are exhibited over three floors, with headphones for visitors to listen to the sounds of the *gaida* (Greek goatskin bagpipes) and Byzantine mandolins, among others. Musical performances are held in the lovely garden in summer. (☏210 325 4119; www.instruments-museum.gr; Diogenous 1-3, Plaka; admission free; ⏱8am-3pm Tue-Sun; Ⓜ Monastiraki)

Greek Folk Art Museum

MUSEUM

9 ◉ Map p62, A3

As of 2015, this superb collection was closed as it began its transition to a new museum site at Adrianou. Once it opens, it will display secular and religious folk art, mainly from the 18th and 19th centuries. Exhibits include embroidery, pottery, weaving and puppets, and a reconstructed traditional village house with paintings by Theophilos. Greek traditional costumes will also be on display. (☏210 322 9031; www.melt.gr; Adrianou & Areos, Plaka; Ⓜ Syntagma)

Eating

2 Mazi   FUSION €€

10 ✗ Map p62, E4

Inside a neoclassical mansion, this elegant dining room with white linen and proper crystal is the venue for inventive creations by two young chefs. They incorporate fresh local products such as mountain greens, Greek cheeses and fresh-caught seafood to make interesting and beautifully presented dishes spanning the cuisines of Asia, France and the Greek islands. (☏210 322 2839; www.2mazi.gr; Nikis 48, Plaka; mains €17-22; ☉1pm-midnight; Ⓜ Syntagma, Akropoli)

Tzitzikas & Mermingas   MEZEDHES €

11 ✗ Map p62, E3

Greek merchandise lines the walls of this cheery, modern *mezedhopoleio* (restaurant specialising in mezedhes) that sits smack in the middle of central Athens. It serves a tasty range of

delicious and creative mezedhes (such as the honey-drizzled, bacon-wrapped Naxos cheese) to a bustling crowd of locals. (☏210 324 7607; www. tzitzikasmermigas.gr; Mitropoleos 12-14, Syntagma; mezedhes €6-12; ☉noon-11pm; Ⓜ Syntagma)

Kalnterimi   TAVERNA €

12 ✗ Map p62, C1

Find your way behind the Church of Agii Theodori to this hidden, open-air taverna offering Greek food at its most authentic. Everything is fresh-cooked and delicious: you can't go wrong. Hand-painted tables spill onto the footpath along a pedestrian street and give a feeling of peace in one of the busiest parts of the city. (☏210 331 0049; www.kalnterimi.gr; Plateia Agion Theodoron, cnr Skouleniou, Monastiraki; mains €5-8; ☉noon-11pm Mon-Sat; ☎; Ⓜ Panepistimio)

Pure Bliss   CAFE €

13 ✗ Map p62, C2

Enjoy the laid-back vibe at one of the few places in Athens where you can get organic fair-trade coffee, exotic teas and soy products. There's a range of healthy salads, sandwiches, smoothies and mostly organic food, wine and cocktails. (☏210 325 0360; www.purebliss.gr; Romvis 24a, Syntagma; snacks €3-9; ☉10.30am-1am Mon-Sat, 5-9pm Sun; ☎✐; Ⓜ Syntagma)

Local Life

Street Snacks

Since 1910 **Ariston** (📞210 322 7626; Voulis 10, Syntagma; pies €1.40-2; 🕙10am-4pm Mon-Fri; Ⓜ Syntagma) has been baking the best fresh *tyropites* (cheese pies), the perfect snack on the run. Try its renowned *kourou* (thick type of pastry) variety or one of the many other tasty fillings, such as red peppers, mushrooms, chicken or spinach.

Glykis   MEZEDHES €

14 🍴 Map p62, D5

In a quiet corner of Plaka, this low-key *mezedhopoleio* with a shady courtyard is mostly frequented by students and locals. It has a tasty selection of mezedhes, including traditional dishes such as *briam* (oven-baked vegetable casserole) and cuttlefish in wine. (📞210 322 3925; Angelou Geronta 2, Plaka; mezedhes €6-8; 🕙10.30am-1.30am; Ⓜ Akropoli)

Paradosiako   TAVERNA €€

15 🍴 Map p62, D4

For great traditional fare, you can't beat this inconspicuous, no-frills taverna on the periphery of Plaka, with a few tables on the footpath. There's a basic menu but it's best to choose from the daily specials, which include fresh seafood such as prawn saganaki.

(📞210 321 4121; Voulis 44a, Plaka; mains €5-12; 🕙lunch & dinner; 📶; Ⓜ Syntagma)

Palia Taverna tou Psara   TAVERNA €€

16 🍴 Map p62, C5

Away from the main hustle of Plaka, this taverna is a cut above the rest and fills tables cascading across the street. It's known as the best seafood taverna in Plaka (fish €65 per kilogram). (📞210 321 8733; www.psaras-taverna.gr; Erechtheos 16, Plaka; mains €12-24; 🕙11am-12.30am Wed-Mon; Ⓜ Akropoli)

Drinking

Clumsies   BAR

17 🍺 Map p62, C1

Warm, welcoming decor with a design-retro feel and a packed, babbling crowd of happy sippers (from coffee to creative cocktail) make this new all-day bar a go-to hangout for locals and visitors alike. (📞210 323 2682; www.theclumsies.gr; Praxitelous 30, Syntagma; 🕙9am-late; Ⓜ Syntagma)

Seven Jokers   BAR

18 🍺 Map p62, E2

Lively and central Seven Jokers anchors a party block, also shared by spacious 42 Bar (p71; around the corner), which serves cocktails in wood-panelled splendour. (📞210 321 9225; Voulis 7, Syntagma; 🕙1pm-late; Ⓜ Syntagma)

Cafes, Plaka

Drunk Sinatra   COCKTAIL BAR

19 🚇 Map p62, D2

Athens' newest hipster hang-out also
serves a mean cocktail. (🗷210 331
3733; Thiseos 16, Syntagma; ⊘10am-late;
Ⓜ Syntagma)

Barley Cargo   BAR

20 🚇 Map p62, D1

This fantastic beer bar offers more
than 150 different versions of the
elixir, many of them from Greek
microbreweries. Or sip a Trappist
brew at one of the wooden-barrel
tables. (🗷210 323 0445; Kolokotroni 6,
Syntagma; ⊘11am-3am; Ⓜ Syntagma)

Brettos   BAR

21 🚇 Map p62, D5

You won't find any happening bars in
Plaka, but Brettos is a delightful old
bar and distillery with a stunning wall
of colourful bottles and huge barrels.
Sample its home brands of wine, ouzo,
brandy and other spirits. (🗷210 323
2110; www.brettosplaka.com; Kydathineon 41,
Plaka; ⊘10am-3am; Ⓜ Akropoli)

Galaxy Bar   BAR

22 🚇 Map p62, E1

Not to be confused with the Hilton's
sky bar, this sweet little wood-panelled
place has a homey saloon feel and
a venerable history. (🗷210 322 7733;

Top Tip

Nightlife

▶ Expect bars to begin filling after 11pm and stay open till late.

▶ With the current strapped financial climate in Athens, watch your back, wherever you go.

▶ For the best dancing in summer, cab it to beach clubs along the coast near Glyfada – city locations close in summer.

Stadiou 10, Syntagma; ⏰1pm-late Mon-Sat; Ⓜ Syntagma)

Bartesera   BAR

23 Ⓞ Map p62, D2

This casual bar-cafe with great music hides out at the end of a narrow arcade. (☎210 322 9805; Kolokotroni 25, Syntagma; ⏰10am-late; Ⓜ Syntagma)

Oinoscent   WINE BAR

24 Ⓞ Map p62, E4

Drop in for a vast array of Greek and international wines, or pick up a bottle for the road. (☎210 322 9374; www. oinoscent.gr; Voulis 45-47, Plaka; ⏰11am-1am; Ⓜ Syntagma)

Sixx   CLUB

25 Ⓞ Map p62, F1

If you just can't call it a night... DJs party till dawn. (☎6979470638;

Amerikis 6, Syntagma; ⏰11pm-7am Fri-Sat; Ⓜ Syntagma)

Klepsydra   CAFE

26 Ⓞ Map p62, A4

Tucked away in a delightfully quiet spot under the Acropolis, with shady outdoor tables and friendly service, Klepsydra is a favourite with locals and an ideal rest spot after serious sightseeing; there's a small selection of snacks, such as *spanakopites* (spinach pies). (☎210 321 2493; Klepsydras & Thrasyvoulou, Plaka; snacks €4; ⏰9am-1am; Ⓜ Monastiraki)

Entertainment

Perivoli tou Ouranou   TRADITIONAL MUSIC

27 ⭐ Map p62, E5

A favourite rustic, old-style Plaka music haunt with dinner (mains €18 to €29). (☎210 323 5517; www.perivoli touranou.gr; Lysikratous 19, Plaka; ⏰9pm-late Thu-Sun, closed Jul-Sep; Ⓜ Akropoli)

Cine Paris   CINEMA

28 ⭐ Map p62, D5

A magical place to see a movie, this traditional old rooftop cinema in Plaka has great views of the Acropolis from some seats. (☎210 322 0721; www.cineparis.gr; Kydathineon 22, Plaka; Ⓜ Syntagma)

Palea Plakiotiki Taverna
Stamatopoulos   TRADITIONAL MUSIC

29 ⭐ Map p62, C4

This Plaka restaurant is an institution, with live music nightly. It fills up late with locals – arrive early for a table. (☎210 322 8722; www.stamatopoulostavern.gr; Lyssiou 26, Plaka; ⏲7pm-2am Mon-Sat, 11am-2am Sun; Ⓜ Monastiraki)

Mostrou   TRADITIONAL MUSIC

30 ⭐ Map p62, B4

There's a popular full-sized stage and dance floor at this restaurant; in summer there's more sedate live music on the terrace. (☎210 322 5558; www.mostrou.gr; Mnisikleous 22, cnr Lyssiou, Plaka; ⏲6pm-2am Thu-Sun; Ⓜ Monastiraki)

Shopping

Aidini   ART, CRAFTS

31 🔒 Map p62, E4

Artisan Errikos Aidini's unique metal creations are made in his workshop at the back of this charming store, including small mirrors, candlesticks, lamps, planes and his signature bronze boats. (☎210 323 4591; Nikis 32, Plaka; ⏲10.30am-5pm Mon & Wed, to 9pm Tue, Thu & Fri, to 4pm Sat; Ⓜ Syntagma)

Apriati   JEWELLERY

32 🔒 Map p62, F2

This tiny, delightful store has a tempting selection of fun and original

contemporary designs from Athena Axioti, Themis Bobolas and other local designers. There are additional shops in Kolonaki and on Ermou. (☎210 322 9183; www.apriati.com; Stadiou 3, Syntagma; ⏲10am-4.30pm Mon, Wed & Sat, to 8.30pm Tue, Thu & Fri; Ⓜ Syntagma)

Korres   BEAUTY

33 🔒 Map p62, E3

You can get the full range from this natural beauty-product guru at the company's original homeopathic pharmacy – at a fraction of the price you'll pay in London or New York. There's also a branch at the airport, and one

Local Life
Party Central

Seek out the areas around Plateia Karytsi and Kolokotroni (north of Syntagma) and Plateia Agia Irini (Monastiraki) for crowds of Athenians out on the town. Psyrri has seen a recent resurgence, while Kolonaki steadfastly attracts the trendier set, and Gazi remains tried-and-true. Around Plateia Karytsi you'll find old favourites, including **Toy** (☎210 331 1555; Plateia Karytsi 10, Syntagma; ⏲noon-4am; Ⓜ Syntagma), where locals gather for coffee by day and booze by night, or **42 Bar** (Kolokotroni 3, Syntagma; ⏲9am-2am; Ⓜ Syntagma), with excellent cocktails in wood-panelled splendour.

near the Panathenaic Stadium. (☎210 321 0054, 213 018 8800; www.korres.com; Ermou 4, Syntagma; ⊗9am-9pm Mon-Fri, to 8pm Sat; Ⓜ Syntagma)

Amorgos
HANDICRAFTS

34 🔒 Map p62, E4

Charming store crammed with Greek folk art, trinkets, ceramics, embroidery and carved wooden furniture made by the owner. (☎210 324 3836; www.amorgosart.gr; Kodrou 3, Plaka; ⊗11am-8pm Mon-Fri, to 7pm Sat; Ⓜ Syntagma)

☑ Top Tip

One-Stop Shopping

Major Greek chains combine lots of wares under one roof. The enormous **Attica** (☎211 180 2500; www.atticadps.gr; Panepistimiou 9, Syntagma; ⊗10am-9pm Mon-Fri, to 7pm Sat; Ⓜ Syntagma) department store has it all, **Eleftheroudakis** (☎210 325 8440; Panepistimiou 15, Syntagma; ⊗9am-9pm Mon-Fri, 10am-4pm Sat; Ⓜ Syntagma) is a bibliophile heaven and **Public** (☎210 324 6210; www.public.gr; Plateia Syntagmatos, Syntagma; ⊗9am-9pm Mon-Fri, to 8pm Sat; 🛜; Ⓜ Syntagma) specialises in computers, stationery and books. Ermou Street is lined with all kinds of major chains.

Xylouris
MUSIC

35 🔒 Map p62, F1

This music treasure trove is run by the family of Cretan musical legend Nikos Xylouris. They can guide you through the comprehensive range of Greek music, including select and rare recordings. Also has a branch at the Museum of Greek Popular Instruments (p66). (☎210 322 2711; www.xilouris.gr; Stoa Pesmatzoglou, Panepistimiou 39, Panepistimio; ⊗9am-4pm Mon, Wed & Sat, to 8pm Tue, Thu & Fri; Ⓜ Syntagma)

Zoumboulakis Gallery
ARTS

36 🔒 Map p62, G2

An excellent range of limited-edition prints and posters by leading Greek artists, including Tsarouhis, Mytara and Fassianos. (☎210 363 4454; www.zoumboulakis.gr; Kriezotou 6, Syntagma; ⊗10am-3pm Mon & Wed, 10am-8pm Tue, Thu & Fri, 11am-4pm Sat; Ⓜ Syntagma)

Actipis
JEWELLERY

37 🔒 Map p62, D2

Elegant jewellery based around smooth pebbles and gleaming silver or raw leather help this art jeweller stand out from the crowd. In summers Spiros Actipis has a shop in Mykonos. (☎210 323 6907; www.actipis.com; Lekka 20, Syntagma; ⊗11.30am-8pm Mon-Fri, to 5pm Sat Nov-Apr; Ⓜ Syntagma)

Zoumboulakis Gallery

Zolotas   JEWELLERY

38 🔒 Map p62, E2

Internationally renowned Zolotas
breathes life into ancient Greece with
replicas of museum pieces, having had
the exclusive rights to make copies of
the real thing since 1972. (📞210 331
3320; www.zolotas.gr; Stadiou 9, Syntagma;
⏰10am-4pm Mon, Wed & Sat, to 7pm Tue, Thu
& Fri; Ⓜ Syntagma)

Anavasi   MAPS, BOOKS

39 🔒 Map p62, E3

Great travel bookshop with an
extensive range of Greece maps and
walking and activity guides. (📞210
321 8104; www.anavasi.gr; Voulis 32, cnr
Apollonos, Syntagma; ⏰9.30am-5.30pm Mon
& Wed, to 8.30pm Tue, Thu & Fri, 10am-4.30pm
Sat; Ⓜ Syntagma)

Cellier   WINE

40 🔒 Map p62, G2

A delectable collection of some of
Greece's best wines and liqueurs, with
knowledgeable staff to explain Greek
varieties and winemakers, and boxed
gift packs. (📞210 361 0040; www.cellier.
gr; Kriezotou 1, Syntagma; ⏰10am-6pm Mon,
Wed & Sat, to 9pm Tue, Thu & Fr, reduced hours
Aug; Ⓜ Syntagma)

Explore

Benaki Museum & Kolonaki

Kolonaki is an adjective as much as a district: it's the neighbourhood that most epitomises the Athenian elite. Undeniably chic, Kolonaki is where old money mixes with the nouveau riche and wannabes. Named after a tiny obscure column in the central Plateia Kolonakiou (Kolonaki Sq), Kolonaki stretches from Syntagma to the foothills of Lykavittos Hill, and is home to popular cafes, restaurants, galleries, museums, boutiques and stylish apartment blocks.

The Sights in a Day

☼ Watch the world go by while fuelling up with coffee on Plateia Kolonakiou or at nearby **Filion** (p85). Once you're sated, head out to three of the best museums in Athens: the **Museum of Cycladic Art** (p83), the **Byzantine & Christian Museum** (p82) and the **Benaki Museum** (p76). These could easily fill your day.

☼ Plan to lunch at the Benaki Museum with its terrace cafe, refreshing garden and Acropolis views. Then the browsing begins. Kolonaki is the haunt of fashionistas, so if haute couture is what you're after, you've come to the right place. Even just visiting stellar jeweller **Fanourakis** (p86) or coutourier **Vassilis Zoulias** (p87) will thrill. Or simply cruise the streets, window-shopping, gallery-hopping and watching Athenians do their thing.

☾ Plan to dine out at one of the local Italian restaurants such as **Capanna** (p84) or **Il Postino** (p84), or people-watch at **Kalamaki Kolonaki** (p85). Then join the fray at the bars and clubs, like those on Plateia Kolonakiou, Ploutarhou street or pedestrianised Haritos street, such as **Mai Tai** (p86).

For a local's day people-watching in Kolonaki, see p78.

◉ Top Sights
Benaki Museum (p76)

◯ Local Life
People-Watching in Kolonaki (p78)

♥ Best of Athens

Museums

Benaki Museum (p76)

Museum of Cycladic Art (p83)

Byzantine & Christian Museum (p82)

National Art Gallery (p83)

Theocharakis Foundation for the Fine Arts & Music (p84)

Cafes

Da Capo (p78)

Filion (p85)

Petite Fleur (p85)

To Tsai (p86)

Getting There

Ⓜ **Metro** Emerge at Evangelismos station (blue line) for the eastern extents of Kolonaki. Syntagma station (blue and red lines) brings you to Kolonaki's western edge. Just walk up Leoforos Vasilissis Sofias and cut in to the north.

Top Sights
Benaki Museum

Greece's finest private museum contains the vast collection of Antonis Benakis, accumulated during 35 years of avid collecting in Europe and Asia. In 1931 he turned the family house into a museum and presented it to the Greek nation. The collection displays an astounding breadth: Bronze Age finds from Mycenae and Thessaly; works by El Greco; ecclesiastical furniture brought from Asia Minor; pottery, copper, silver and woodwork from Egypt, Asia Minor and Mesopotamia; and a stunning collection of Greek regional costumes.

👁 Map p80, C5

📞 210 367 1000

www.benaki.gr

Koumbari 1, cnr Leoforos Vasilissis Sofias, Kolonaki

adult/child €7/free, Thu free

🕑 9am-5pm Wed & Fri, to midnight Thu & Sat, to 3pm Sun

Ⓜ Syntagma, Evangelismos

Don't Miss

Earliest Finds
Make sure you pass by the cases in room one on the ground floor to see flint flakes from the Middle Paleolithic period: at 50,000–40,000 BC they may be the oldest human-made thing you ever see.

Ground Floor: Hordes of Treasure
Take your time on the ground floor, where priceless displays range from inscribed golden tablets to Byzantine mosaics, fragile Coptic tapestries, Mycenaean gold jewellery, regal funerary urns and 6th-century gold bracelets from Cyprus.

Costumes
On the 1st floor, prepare to be wowed by a seemingly endless sequence of native dress, from islands all over Greece and on into the Peloponnese, Epiros, Macedonia and Thrace. The spacious displays are interspersed with other priceless objects, like carved marble door frames and jewel-encrusted Ottoman crowns.

Reception Halls
Amazingly, Benaki collected entire rooms: inlaid ceilings, marble floors, antique benches. Two particularly striking examples are the reception hall of the Voulgaris Manision in Hydra (a gift of Pasha Gazi-Hassam) and a mid-18th-century hall from Kazani, Macedonia.

Cretan School Painters
Painters in Venetian-held Crete (15th–16th centuries) developed a signature icon-painting style. The Benaki holds masterpieces of the genre in room 12, which includes work by Domenikos Theotokopoulos (El Greco, 1541–1614), and several by Theodoros Poulakis (1622–1692), in room 27.

☑ Top Tips

▶ The Benaki has expanded into several equally exemplary branches to house its vast, diverse collections, which host a full schedule of rotating exhibitions, posted on its website.

▶ The Benaki Museum Pireos Annexe (p129), in an impressive former industrial building, is tops for art.

▶ The Museum of Islamic Art (p129) holds a top-notch collection.

✖ Take a Break

The Benaki's cafe (mains €12–€16) is renowned to for great food in an open dining room, stretching out onto a terrace overlooking the national gardens and the Acropolis. Locals often come to the museum just for lunch!

Otherwise, pop over to Plateia Kolonakiou to a cafe such as Da Capo (p78).

Local Life
People-Watching in Kolonaki

On Plateia Kolonakiou you'll find the original people-watching cafes teeming with yuppies, actors, politicians, journalists and a passing parade of aristocratic Athenian ladies, style queens and glitzy fashion victims. The cool younger set frequents the bars on Skoufa, Haritos and Ploutarhou. Join the flow for what Kolonaki has always been – good, solid fun and fashionability.

1 Coffee Klatch

A Kolonaki pastime is the extended people-perusing coffee session. Try iconic **Da Capo** (☎210 360 2497; Tsakalof 1, Kolonaki; ⏰8am-7pm; Ⓜ Syntagma), which anchors the cafes on the main square and is *the* place to be seen. (It's self-serve if you can find a table.)

2 Designer Shopping

Kolonaki is Athens' boutique epi-centre, and fashionistas go Greek and

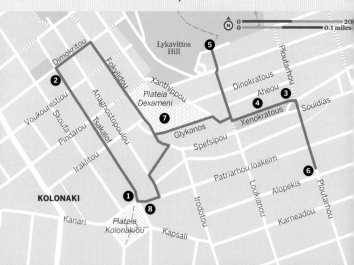

totally natural at **Parthenis** (📞210 363 3158; www.orsalia-parthenis.gr; Dimokritou 20, cnr Tsakalof, Kolonaki; ⊙10am-3pm Mon & Wed, to 8.30pm Tue, Thu & Fri, to 4pm Sat; Ⓜ Syntagma), where a father-and-daughter team offer classic silhouettes in natural fibres.

❸ Traditional Taverna

Filippou (📞210 721 6390; Xenokratous 19, Kolonaki; mains €8-12; ⊙1-5pm & 7-11pm Mon-Fri, 1-5pm Sat; Ⓜ Evangelismos) is always packed with locals enjoying the renowned home-style fare that this classic taverna has been dishing out since 1923. White-linen-covered tables spill into the courtyard, but book ahead to ensure you get one.

❹ Art Galleries

Join art connoisseurs at **Medusa Art Gallery** (📞210 724 4552; www.medusaart gallery.com; Xenokratous 7, Kolonaki; ⊙11am-2.30pm & 6.30-9.30pm Tue-Fri, closed Aug; Ⓜ Evangelismos), which has focused for over 30 years on excellent Greek contemporary painting, sculpture, installations and photography.

❺ Climb Lykavittos Hill

A path leads to the summit of Lykavittos Hill from the top of Loukianou for the finest panoramas of the city and the Attic basin – the *nefos* (pollution haze) permitting. Alternatively, take the **teleferik** (funicular railway; 📞210 721 0701; ⊙9am-3am, runs every 30min; return €6) from the top of Ploutarhou

in Kolonaki. Perched on the summit is the little Chapel of Agios Georgios, floodlit like a beacon over the city at night.

❻ Super Streetside Dinner

Watch the jet set head out for the night, streetside at **Oikeio** (📞210 725 9216; Ploutarhou 15, Kolonaki; mains €7-14; ⊙1pm-2.30am Mon-Sat; Ⓜ Evangelismos). With excellent home-style cooking, this modern taverna lives up to its name (meaning 'homey'). It's decorated like a cosy bistro on the inside, and tables on the pavement allow people-watching without the normal Kolonaki bill. Book ahead, as it always fills up.

❼ Cinema Under the Stars

Things in Kolonaki get more sedate in the streets towards Lykavittos. The classic open-air cinema, **Dexameni** (📞210 362 3942; www.cinedexameni.gr; Plateia Dexameni, Kolonaki; Ⓜ Evangelismos), is in a lovely spot up on Plateia Dexameni, with a wall of cascading bougainvillea, deck chairs and little tables to rest your beer on.

❽ Dress to Kill

Join the beautiful young things at **Rock'n'Roll** (📞210 722 0649; Plateia Kolonakiou, Kolonaki; ⊙Sep-Jun; Ⓜ Evangelismos), a Kolonaki classic that lives up to its name. Saturday dance parties get wild, and each night has different DJ'd sets.

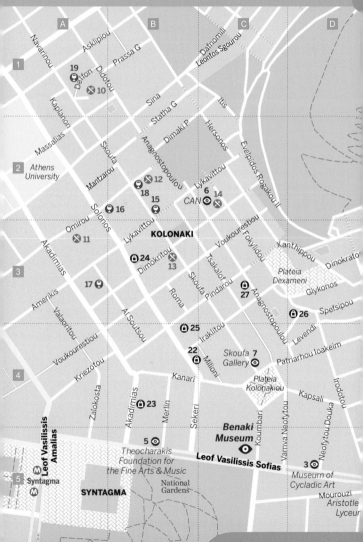

E   F   G   H

Lykavittos Hill

0   200 m
0   0.1 miles

Athineon Efivon

Karahristou

Dimoharous

Dinokratous

Hoida

Doras D'Istria

Aristippou

Aristodimou

Iroflou

Kleomenous

Dinokratous

Xenokratous

Plateia
Dante

Evzonon

ou

okratous

Souidias

Genadiou I

Iasiou

Monis Petraki

Haritos

⊗9

Patera I

Ravine

21

Patriarhou Ioakeim

Ypsilandou

Leof Vasilissis Sofias

Alopekis

20
🅿

Marasli

Ploutarhou

Karneadou

Plateia
Megalis tou
Genous Sholi

Venturik

anou

Ypsilandou

Evangelismos Ⓜ

Ⓜ

Vasilissis Sofias

Leof Vas Konstantinou

Leof Vasileos Alexandrou

4 ⊙
National
Art Gallery

Mihalakopoulou

1 ⊙
Byzantine &
Christian
Museum

Rizari

Plateia
Madritis
⊗8

Vrasida

For reviews see	
⊙ Top Sights	p76
⊙ Sights	p82
⊗ Eating	p84
🍷 Drinking	p85
🛍 Shopping	p86

Understand
Byzantine Athens

With the rise of the Byzantine Empire, which blended Hellenistic culture with Christianity, the Greek city of Byzantium (renamed Constantinople in AD 330, present-day İstanbul) became the capital of the Roman Empire headed by the Roman Emperor Constantine I, a Christian convert. While Rome went into terminal decline, this eastern capital began to grow in wealth and strength as a Christian state. In the ensuing centuries Byzantine Greece faced continued pressure from the Persians and Arabs, but it retained its hold over the region.

Christianity was made the official religion of Greece in 394, and worship of Greek and Roman gods was banned. Athens remained an important cultural centre until 529, when the teaching of 'pagan' classical philosophy was forbidden in favour of Christian theology. From 1200 to 1450 Athens was occupied by a succession of opportunistic invaders – Franks, Catalans, Florentines and Venetians. By the time it was chosen as the new Greek capital in 1834, it was little more than a dusty outpost of the Byzantine Empire.

The Byzantine Empire outlived Rome, lasting until the Turks captured Constantinople in 1453.

Sights

Byzantine & Christian Museum   MUSEUM

1 ◉ Map p80, E5

This outstanding museum – on the grounds of former Villa Ilissia, an urban oasis – presents a priceless collection of Christian art from the 3rd to 20th centuries. Thematic snapshots of the Byzantine and post-Byzantine world are exceptionally presented in expansive, well-lit, multilevel galleries, clearly arranged chronologically with English translations. The collection includes icons, frescoes, sculptures, textiles, manuscripts, vestments and mosaics. (☎213 213 9500; www.byzantinemuseum.gr; Leoforos Vasilissis Sofias 22, Kolonaki; adult/child €4/free; ◷8am-8pm Apr-Oct, reduced hours Nov-Mar; ⓂEvangelismos)

Aristotle's Lyceum   RUIN

2 ◉ Map p80, D5

The Lyceum where Aristotle founded his school in 335 BC has opened to the public after years of archaeological work; admission to the site is free. The Lyceum, which used to lie outside the city walls, was a *gymnasium* where Aristotle taught rhetoric and philosophy. It was also known as a Peripatetic School, because teacher and pupils would walk as they talked.

Museum of Cycladic Art

(cnr Rigillis & Leof Vasilissis Sofias; admission free; ☺8am-8pm Mon-Fri; Ⓜ Evangelismos)

Museum of Cycladic Art   MUSEUM

3 ◉ Map p80, D5

This exceptional private museum boasts the largest independent collection of distinctive Cycladic art and holds excellent periodic exhibitions of all sorts. The 1st-floor Cycladic collection, dating from 3000 BC to 2000 BC, includes the marble figurines that inspired many 20th-century artists, such as Picasso and Modigliani, with their simplicity and purity of form. The rest of the museum features Greek and Cypriot art dating from

2000 BC to the 4th century AD. (✆210 722 8321; www.cycladic.gr; Neofytou Douka 4, cnr Leoforos Vasilissis Sofias, Kolonaki; adult/child €7/free, Mon half-price; ☺10am-5pm Mon, Wed, Fri & Sat, to 8pm Thu, 11am-5pm Sun; Ⓜ Evangelismos)

National Art Gallery   GALLERY

4 ◉ Map p80, G5

Greece's national art museum presents a rich collection of Greek art spanning four centuries from the post-Byzantine period. The newer wing houses its permanent collection and traces the key art movements chronologically. At the time of writing, the museum was closed for refurbishment. (✆210 723 5937; www.nationalgallery.gr;

Leoforos Vasileos Konstantinou 50, Kolonaki;
Ⓜ Evangelismos)

Theocharakis Foundation for the Fine Arts & Music

GALLERY

5 ◉ Map p80, B5

This excellent centre has three levels
of exhibition space featuring local and
international 20th- and 21st-century
artists, a theatre, an art shop and a
pleasant cafe. Music performances
are held between September and May.
(☎ 210 361 1206; www.thf.gr; Leoforos Vasilissis Sofias 9, Kolonaki; adult/child €6/free;
⊙ 10am-6pm Mon-Wed & Fri-Sun, to 8pm Thu,
closed Aug; 🛜; Ⓜ Syntagma)

CAN

GALLERY

6 ◉ Map p80, C2

The brainchild of Christina Androuli-
daki, this recent entry on the Kolonaki
gallery scene is building a stable of
emerging contemporary Greek artists.
(☎ 210 339 0833; www.can-gallery.com;
Anagnostopoulou 42, Kolonaki; ⊙ 11am-3pm
& 5-8pm Tue-Fri, 11am-4pm Sat, closed Aug;
Ⓜ Syntagma)

Skoufa Gallery

GALLERY

7 ◉ Map p80, C4

A long-standing anchor of contemporary Greek artists just off Plateia
Kolonakiou. (☎ 210 364 3025; www.
skoufagallery.gr; Skoufa 4, Kolonaki; ⊙ 10am-
3.30pm Mon, Wed & Sat, 5.30-9pm Tue, Thu &
Fri; Ⓜ Syntagma)

Eating

Alatsi

CRETAN €€

8 ✗ Map p80, H5

Alatsi represents the new breed of
trendy upscale restaurants, serving
traditional Cretan cuisine, such as
gamopilafo (wedding pilaf) with lamb
or rare *stamnagathi* (wild greens), to
fashionable Athenians. The excellent menu changes seasonally. Book
ahead. You'll find it near the Hilton.
(☎ 210 721 0501; www.alatsi.gr; Vrasida 13,
Ilissia; mains €12-18; ⊙ 1pm-1am Mon-Sat;
Ⓜ Evangelismos)

Capanna

ITALIAN €€

9 ✗ Map p80, E3

Capanna hugs a Kolonaki corner, with
tables wrapping around the footpath
in summer. Cuisine is fresh Italian,
from enormous pizzas to gnocchi
with Gorgonzola. Enjoy hearty eating
with attentive service and a goblet of
wine, though prices are a tad high.
(☎ 210 724 1777; Ploutarhou 38 & Haritos 42,
Kolonaki; mains €10-17; ⊙ 1pm-1am Tue-Sun;
🛜; Ⓜ Evangelismos)

Il Postino

ITALIAN €€

10 ✗ Map p80, A1

In the mood for a plate of homemade
gnocchi with pesto before a night out
clubbing? Sneak into this little side
street and sup under old photos of
Roma. (☎ 210 364 1414; Grivaion 3, Kolonaki;
pasta €8-12; ⊙ 1-11.30pm; Ⓜ Panepistimio)

Café Boheme
CAFE €€

11 Map p80, A3

A jazzy, brasserie-like spot, it also has a great wine selection and serves everything from sandwiches and salads to rib-eye steak (€19.50). (210 360 8018; www.cafeboheme.gr; Omirou 36, Kolonaki; mains €6.50-15; 10.30am-late Mon-Fri, from noon Sat & Sun; Panepistimiou)

Nice N' Easy
CAFE €

12 Map p80, B2

Dig into organic, fresh sandwiches, salads and brunch treats such as huevos rancheros beneath images of Louis Armstrong and Marilyn Monroe at this casual cafe. (210 361 7201; www.niceneasy.gr; Omirou 60, Kolonaki; sandwiches €5-10; 9am-1.30am; ; Panepistimio)

Loukoumelo
DESSERTS €

13 Map p80, B3

This friendly storefront specialises in loukoumadhes, a Greek style of doughnut, served warm and with all sort of flavours. Pair it with ice cream to get really decadent. (211 012 5330; www.loukoumelo.gr; Skoufa 37, Kolonaki; sweets €2.70-3.80; 8.30am-11pm Mon-Fri, 9.30am-midnight Sat & Sun; Syntagma)

Papadakis
SEAFOOD €€

14 Map p80, C2

This understatedly chic restaurant specialises in creative seafood, like stewed octopus with honey and sweet

Local Life
Streetside Souvlaki

Kolonaki's stand-out souvlaki joint, **Kalamaki Kolonaki** (210 721 8800; Ploutarhou 32, Kolonaki; mains €7; 1pm-midnight; Evangelismos) still manages to retain that Kolonaki aplomb. Order by the kalamaki (skewer, €1.70), and add on some salad and pittas, and you've got great quick eats with all the requisite people-watching.

wine, salatouri (fish salad) and sea salad (a type of green seaweed/ sea asparagus). Service can be snooty. (210 360 8621; Fokylidou 15, Kolonaki; mains €18-38; 1.30pm-midnight Mon-Sat; Syntagma)

Drinking

Filion
CAFE

15 Map p80, B2

Despite its unassuming decor, Filion consistently attracts the intellectual set: artists, writers and film-makers. (210 361 2850; Skoufa 34, Kolonaki; 8am-midnight; Syntagma)

Petite Fleur
CAFE

16 Map p80, B2

Petite Fleur serves up large mugs of hot chocolate and speciality cappuccinos in a quiet, almost-Parisian ambience. (www.petite-fleur.gr; Omirou 44, Kolonaki; 8am-11pm; Panepistimio)

To Tsai

TEAHOUSE

17 Map p80, A3

Get a Zen vibe as you sip tea at natural-wood tables; on a lively day, a bit of Dixieland jazz will be tinkling in the background. Light meals (€6 to €9) include soup and grilled chicken. (210 338 8941; www.tea.gr; Alexandrou Soutsou 19, Kolonaki; 6am-9pm Mon-Sat, daily in winter; Syntagma)

Rosebud

BAR

18 Map p80, B2

Kolonaki professionals and chicsters cram this cocktail bar, which also offers vegetarian food. (210 339 2370; www.rosebud.gr; Omirou 60, cnr Skoufa, Kolonaki; 9.30am-1.30am; ; Panepistimiou)

Mommy

BAR

19 Map p80, A1

Tucked way back in a side street off busy Skoufa, Mommy is popular for English-speaking locals and its weekly '80s night. (210 361 9682; Delfon 4, Kolonaki; noon-midnight; Panepistimiou)

Mai Tai

BAR

20 Map p80, E4

Join Kolonaki's best dressed as they pack into this narrow bar and spill out into the street beyond. It's a place to see and be seen. (210 722 5846; Ploutarhou 18, Kolonaki; noon-late; Evangelismos)

Shopping

Fanourakis

JEWELLERY

21 Map p80, E3

One of the most creative, exciting Greek jewellers, Fanourakis designs delicate pieces of folded gold, encrusted rings, bows, and other unique creations. The distinctive forms are sheer art, a factor that is also reflected in the prices (though it now has a more inexpensive line as well). (210 721 1762; www.fanourakis.gr; Patriarhou Ioakeim 23, Kolonaki; 10am-5pm Mon, Wed & Sat, to 9pm Tue, Thu & Fri; Syntagma)

Apivita

BEAUTY

22 Map p80, B4

Apivita's flagship store has the full range of its excellent natural beauty products and an express spa downstairs for pampering on the run. There's also a branch at the airport. (210 364 0560; www.apivita.com; Solonos

Local Life
Haritos Street

The hopping pedestrianised end of Haritos is lined with bars and is a popular spot for the younger set; most nights folks spill out on to the road, drinking on the steps of the apartment blocks opposite. Or head to the end of the street to **Cine Athinaia** (210 721 5717; Haritos 50, Kolonaki; Evangelismos) for a summertime open-air movie.

6, Kolonaki; ⏰10am-9pm Tue, Thu & Fri, to 5pm Mon, Wed & Sat, spa closed Mon & Sun; Ⓜ Syntagma)

Vassilis Zoulias   CLOTHING, SHOES

23 🔒 Map p80, B4

An exquisite range of elegant, feminine shoes can be found at the boutique store of Greece's Manolo Blahnik. Some of these designs are works of art inspired by '50s and '60s films, as is his couture line. (☎210 338 9924; www.vassiliszoulias.com; Akadimias 4, Kolonaki; ⏰10am-5pm Mon, Wed & Sat, to 9pm Tue, Thu & Fri; Ⓜ Syntagma)

Graffito   GIFTS

24 🔒 Map p80, B3

A new entry on the Athens shopping scene, Graffito combines homewares, fashion and other high-design items with a welcoming cafe. (☎210 360 8936; www.graffito.gr; Solonos 34, Kolonaki; ⏰8am-9pm; Ⓜ Panepistimio, Syntagma)

Gusto di Grecia   FOOD, DRINK

25 🔒 Map p80, B4

Shop for the best treats from all over Greece, from cheese to local honeys, cold cuts, olive oil and wine. (☎210 362 6809; Pindarou 16-20, Kolonaki; ⏰8am-10pm Mon-Sat; Ⓜ Syntagma)

Elena Votsi   JEWELLERY

26 🔒 Map p80, D3

Votsi is renowned for her original, big and bold designs using exquisite semi-

precious stones. Her work also sells in New York and London, and her profile got a big boost when she was chosen to design the new Olympic Games medal. (☎210 360 0936; www.elenavotsi. com; Xanthou 7, Kolonaki; ⏰10am-8pm Tue-Sat; Ⓜ Evangelismos)

Bettina   CLOTHING

27 🔒 Map p80, C3

This chic boutique carries top-name fashion, including creations by Greek fashion queen Sophia Kokosalaki, Angelos Frentzos and other well-known local and international designers. (☎210 339 2094; www.bettina.com.gr; Anagnostopoulou 29, Kolonaki; ⏰10am-3.30pm Mon, Wed & Sat, to 8pm Tue, Thu & Fri; Ⓜ Syntagma)

Explore

Temple of Olympian Zeus & Panathenaic Stadium

To the east of the Acropolis, the Zappeio Gardens and the ruins of the Temple of Olympian Zeus lead to the elegant Panathenaic Stadium (pictured, above), built into Ardettos Hill. The attractive residential district Mets, characterised by some delightful neoclassical and prewar houses, runs up and behind the stadium. Northeast of Mets, Pangrati is a diverse residential neighbourhood with interesting music clubs, cafes and old-style family-run tavernas.

The Sights in a Day

☀️ Take a gander at the enormous **Temple of Olympian Zeus** (p90), which took more than 700 years to build, and read Hadrian's inscription on nearby **Hadrian's Arch** (p91), then head over to the spectacular marble **Panathenaic Stadium** (p94) to see the site of the first modern Olympics.

☀️ Unwind under the shade trees with Athens' best pizza at **Colibri** (p96), then walk it off at **Athens' First Cemetery** (p94), where Greek luminaries are buried in elaborate tombs. Or repose at the lush **Zappeio Gardens** (p95) and nosh on simple dishes at its **Aigli Cafe** (p96).

🌙 Dinner will be a challenge: choose between the authentic Greek **Aigli Restaurant** (p96), the popular modern Greek *mezedhopoleio* (restaurant specialising in mezedhes) **Mavro Provato** (p95), or perhaps one of Athens' very best restaurants, **Spondi** (p95), with a French twist. Finish the night out with live music at Athens' premier jazz venue, the **Half Note Jazz Club** (p96). Alternatively, watch a movie under the stars at the **Aigli Cinema** (p97).

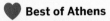 **Top Sights**

Temple of Olympian Zeus (p90)

💜 **Best of Athens**

Top Archaeological Sites
Panathenaic Stadium (p94)

Hadrian's Arch (p91)

Food
Spondi (p95)

Mavro Provato (p95)

Entertainment
Half Note Jazz Club (p96)

Aigli Cinema (p97)

Getting There

Ⓜ**Metro** To reach the Temple of Olympian Zeus use the Akropoli station (red line) or, closer to Zappeio Gardens, the Syntagma station (blue and red lines).

🚎**Trolleybus** To get as close to Pangrati or Mets as possible take trolleybus 2, 4 or 11. Or walk over from the metro – about 15 minutes.

Top Sights
Temple of Olympian Zeus

You can't miss this striking marvel, smack in the centre of Athens. Also known as the Olympeion, it is the largest temple in Greece and, as the name suggests, was dedicated to the supreme god Zeus. Peisistratos began building the temple in the 6th century BC on the western bank of the Ilissos River, but construction stalled due to a lack of funds. A succession of leaders tried to finish the job; Hadrian finally completed the task in AD 131.

Olympieion

👁 Map p92, A2

☎ 210 922 6330

http://odysseus.culture.gr

cnr Leoforos Vasilissis Olgas & Leoforos Vasilissis Amalias, Syntagma

🕗 8am-8pm Apr-Oct, 8.30am-3pm Nov-Mar

Ⓜ Akropoli, Syntagma

Don't Miss

Temple

The colossal Temple of Olympian Zeus took more than 700 years to build. When Hadrian finally completed it in AD 131 he put one of the largest statues in the world – a giant gold and ivory statue of Zeus – in the cella and, in typically immodest fashion, placed an equally large one of himself next to it. The temple was pillaged by Barbarian invaders in the the 3rd century AD and later fell into disuse.

Columns

The temple is impressive for the sheer size of its 104 Corinthian columns (17m high with a base diameter of 1.7m), of which 15 remain. Imagine the whole array and you'll get an idea of how grand a site this was. The fallen column was blown down in a gale in 1852.

Original Temple

The Olympeion is built on the site of a smaller temple (590–560 BC), which was dedicated to the cult of Olympian Zeus. Look closely: its foundations can still be seen on the site.

Hadrian's Arch

Just alongside the temple, and free to peruse, sits this lofty monument of Pentelic marble that stands where busy Leoforos Vasilissis Olgas and Leoforos Vasilissis Amalias meet. Roman Emperor Hadrian erected it in AD 132, probably to commemorate the consecration of the temple. The inscriptions show that it was also intended as a dividing point between the ancient and Roman cities. The northwest frieze reads, 'This is Athens, the Ancient city of Theseus', while the southeast frieze states, 'This is the city of Hadrian, and not of Theseus'.

☑ Top Tips

▶ Admission is included in the €12 Acropolis entry ticket, otherwise adult/child €2/free

▶ There is no shade: wear a hat and sunscreen, bring water.

▶ What you see is what you get – you can peruse the temple (and Hadrian's Arch) from outside if you're in a rush.

✗ Take a Break

For a shady rest and a bit of nourishment, head to the verdant Zappeio Garden's Aegli Cafe (p96).

Or stroll over to Mets, a bit further afield, for a laid-back coffee at the Odeon Cafe (p96).

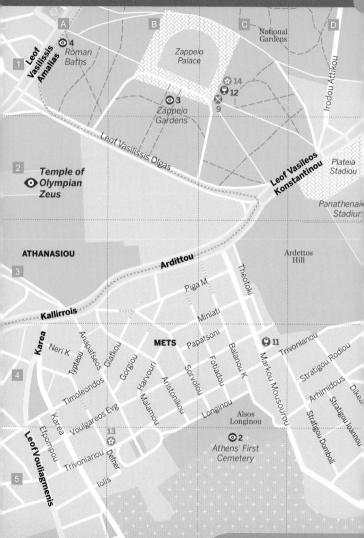

A

B

C

D

1

Leof Vasilissis Amalias

4 Roman Baths

Zappeio Palace

National Gardens

Irodou Attikou

14
12
9

3 Zappeio Gardens

Leof Vasilissis Olgas

Temple of Olympian Zeus

2

Leof Vasileos Konstantinou

Plateia Stadiou

Panathenaic Stadium

ATHANASIOU

3

Ardittou

Ardettos Hill

Kallirrois

Piga M

Theotoki

Karea

Neri K

Anapafseos

Glafkou

Miniati

Papatsoni

METS

Trivonianou

11

Stratigou Rodiou

4

Typteou

Gorgiou

Harvouri

Sorvolou

Fotiadou

Balanou K

Markou Mousourou

Arhimidou

Timoleondos

Malamou

Aristonikou

Longinou

Stratigou Ioannou

Stratigou Domboli

Voulgareos Evg

Karea

Alsos Longinou

2 *Athens' First Cemetery*

Dike

Leof Vouliagmenis

Efpompou

13

Trivonianou

Defner

5

Iolis

E — Leof Vasileos Konstantinou
Fokianou
Ag Spyridonos
Arktinou
Ironda
Patsaniou
Arrianou
Teisesis
Polemonos

F

G
6
N
0   200 m
0   0.1 miles

H

For reviews see
Top Sights	p90
Sights	p94
Eating	p95
Drinking	p96
Entertainment	p96
Shopping	p97

Efforionos
Ivikou
Agras
Versi
Ktisviou
Diofandou
Ironos
Fedrou
Ellanikou

Theofrastou
Eratosthenous
Aristoxenou
Ippodamou
Athanasias
Nikosthenous
Alsos
Pangratiou
Spyrou Merkouri

Tsiklitira
Agras
Plateia
Plastira
Eftyhidou

Arhimidous
Arafou
10
Lysippou
Pastelous
Frynis

PANGRATI
Arhyta
8
Proklou
Pyrgotelous
Effranoros
Tydeos
Vryaxidos
Ymittou
Pyrrou

Ferekydou
Embedokleous
Krisila
Melissou
Plateia
Profiti
Ilia

Parmenidou
Proeresiou
Stilponos
Plateia
Varnava
Korivou
Neoptolemou
Anakreondos
Alketou

Stilponos
Epimitheos
Pyrrou
Pyrronos
Stilponos
Edesiou
Ekalis
Anarhidos
Embedokleous
Damareos
Argyrou

tomachou
5

P 15

Understand
Olympic History

The Olympic tradition emerged at the site of Olympia in the Peloponnese around the 11th century BC as a paean to Zeus, in the form of contests, attended initially by notable men and women who assembled before the sanctuary priests and swore to uphold solemn oaths. By the 8th century attendance had grown and the festival morphed into a male-only major event lasting five days every four years. During the competition, city-states were bound by a sacred truce to stop any fighting underway. The games ceased in AD 394 when Emperor Theodosius I banned them.

Crowds of spectators lined the tracks, where competitors vied for an honourable (and at times dishonourable) victory in athletics, chariot races, wrestling and boxing (no gloves, just simple leather straps). First prize was often a simple laurel wreath, but it was the esteem of the people that most mattered, for Greek Olympians were venerated. Three millennia later, while the scale and scope of the games may have expanded considerably, the basic format is essentially unchanged.

Sights

Panathenaic Stadium

HISTORIC SITE

1 ◎ Map p92, D2

The grand Panathenaic Stadium lies between two pine-covered hills between the neighbourhoods of Mets and Pangrati. It was originally built in the 4th century BC as a venue for the Panathenaic athletic contests. It's said that at Hadrian's inauguration in AD 120, 1000 wild animals were sacrificed in the arena. Later, the seats were rebuilt in Pentelic marble by Herodes Atticus. There are seats for 70,000 spectators, a running track and a central area for field events. (☑210 752 2984; www.panathenaicstadium.gr; Leoforos Vasileos Konstantinou, Pangrati; adult/child €5/2.50; ☉8am-7pm Mar-Oct, to 5pm Nov-Feb; Ⓜ Akropoli)

Athens' First Cemetery

CEMETERY

2 ◎ Map p92, C5

This resting place of many famous Greeks and philhellenes is a peaceful spot to explore. Famous names include the archaeologist Heinrich Schliemann (1822–90), whose mausoleum is decorated with scenes from the Trojan War. Most of the tombstones and mausoleums are lavish in the extreme. Works of art include Halepas' *Sleeping Maiden* sculpture, set on the tomb of a young girl. (Longinou, Mets; ☉7.30am-sunset; Ⓜ Syngrou-Fix)

Zappeio Gardens GARDENS

3 ⦿ Map p92, B1

These gardens sit between the National Gardens and the Panathenaic Stadium and are laid out in a network of wide walkways around the grand Zappeio Palace. The palace was built in the 1870s and hosts conferences and exhibitions. A pleasant cafe, restaurant and the open-air Aigli cinema (p97) are alongside the palace. (entrances on Leoforos Vasilissis Amalias & Leoforos Vasilissis Olgas, Syntagma; Ⓜ Syntagma)

Roman Baths RUIN

4 ⦿ Map p92, A1

Excavation work to create a ventilation shaft for the metro uncovered the well-preserved ruins of a large Roman bath complex. The baths, which extend into the National Gardens, were established near the Ilissos river after the Herulian raids in the 3rd century AD; they were destroyed and repaired again in the 5th or 6th century. (Leoforos Vasilissis Amalias, Syntagma; admission free; Ⓜ Syntagma)

Eating

Spondi MEDITERRANEAN €€€

5 ✗ Map p92, F4

Two-Michelin--starred Spondi is frequently voted Athens' best restaurant, and the accolades are deserved. It offers Mediterranean haute cuisine,

with heavy French influences, in a relaxed, chic setting in a charming old house. Choose from the menu or a range of set dinner and wine *prix fixes*. (📞 210 756 4021; www.spondi.gr; Pyrronos 5, Pangrati; mains €38-50, set menus from €69; ⏰ 8pm-late)

Mavro Provato MEZEDHES €

6 ✗ Map p92, G1

Book ahead for this wildly popular modern *mezedhopoleio* in Pangrati, where tables line the footpath and delicious small plates are paired with *raki* (Cretan firewater) or *tsipouro* (distilled spirit similar to ouzo but usually stronger). (📞 210 722 3466; www.tomauro provato.gr; Arrianou 31-33, Pangrati; dishes €4-12; ⏰ lunch & dinner; Ⓜ Evangelismos)

Trapezaria MODERN GREEK €€

7 ✗ Map p92, E1

In an unassuming spot, this stylish contemporary Greek restaurant packs in locals in search of good, affordable eats, served with style. The wine list is remarkable. (📞 210 921 3500; www.

Local Life

Pangrati

Pangrati's **Plateia Varnava** is a great place to experience a typical Athenian neighbourhood, with families dining in the tavernas and kids playing in the square. The main shopping drag is on the streets leading up to and along **Ymittou**, which has a thriving cafe strip.

trapezaria.gr; Efforionos 13, Pangrati; mains €8-15; ⏱7pm-midnight Tue-Sat, 1-6pm Sun; Ⓜ Evangelismos, Akropoli)

Colibri
PIZZA €

8 Ⓧ Map p92, F4

Locals will tell you this is the best pizza in Athens. While chilling out on a quiet, tree-lined residential street with reggae wafting from inside the restaurant, order from a vast array of classic, vegetarian and gourmet pies, or from a menu of pasta, burgers and salads. (☎210 701 1011; Embedokleous 9-13, Kallimarmaro, Mets; small pizzas €6-12, mains €5-9; ⏱noon-late; 🚌2, 4, 11)

Aigli Restaurant
MEZEDHES €€

9 Ⓧ Map p92, C1

Smack in the heart of the green Zappeio Gardens and next to the palace. Join the crowds tucking into traditional mezedhes and mains, which range from dolmades to marinated anchovies or mushroom risotto. Reservations recommended; in summer aim for the alfresco tables. (☎210 336 9364; www.aeglizappiou.gr; Zappeio Gardens; mezedhes €5-9; ⏱noon-1am; Ⓜ Syntagma, Akropoli)

Vyrinis
TAVERNA €

10 Ⓧ Map p92, F3

Just behind the old Panathenaic stadium, this popular neighbourhood taverna has had a modern makeover but maintains its essence and prices. It has a lovely courtyard garden, simple traditional fare and decent house wine. (☎210 701 2021; Arhimidous 11, Pangrati; mains €6-8; ⏱7-11pm Mon-Fri, noon-3pm & 7-11pm Sat & Sun; 🚌2, 4, 11 to Plateia Plastira)

Drinking

Odeon Cafe
CAFE

11 🍷 Map p92, C4

This delightful slice of local life is a simple corner coffee shop where quietly chatting friends sit beneath ivy hanging over the footpath. Occasional live music. (☎210 922 3414; Markou Mousourou 19, Mets; ⏱8.30am-late; Ⓜ Akropoli)

Aigli Cafe
CAFE, BAR

12 🍷 Map p92, C1

A stylish and cool (literally) cafe-bar-restaurant set among the trees in the middle of the Zappeio Gardens, with comfy loungers and ever-changing decor. It's a low-key cafe by day, while at night it boasts mainstream music and a slick crowd. Food is basic. (☎210 336 9340; Zappeio Gardens; ⏱9am-midnight; Ⓜ Syntagma)

Entertainment

Half Note Jazz Club
JAZZ

13 ⭐ Map p92, B5

Athens' stylish, principal and most serious jazz venue hosts an array of international musicians. (☎210 921 3310; www.halfnote.gr; Trivonianou 17, Mets; Ⓜ Akropoli)

Understand
Peisistratos the Dictator

By the 6th century BC, Athens was ruled by aristocrats and generals. Labourers and peasants had no rights until Solon, the harbinger of Athenian democracy, became *arhon* (chief magistrate) in 594 BC and improved the lot of the poor, with reforms such as the annulment of debts and the implementation of trial by jury. Continuing unrest over the reforms created the pretext for the tyrant Peisistratos, formerly head of the military, to seize power in 560 BC.

Peisistratos built a formidable navy and extended the boundaries of Athenian influence. A patron of the arts, he inaugurated the Festival of the Great Dionysia, the precursor of Attic drama, and commissioned many splendid works, most of which were destroyed by the Persians. He also initiated the enormous project of building the Temple of Olympian Zeus.

Peisistratos was succeeded by his son, Hippias, in 528 BC; Athens rid itself of this oppressor in 510 BC with the help of Sparta.

Aigli Cinema   CINEMA

14 ⭐ Map p92, C1

Historic open-air cinema in the verdant Zappeio Gardens. (📞210 336 9369; www.aeglizappiou.gr; Zappeio Gardens, Syntagma; Ⓜ Syntagma)

Shopping

Bakaniko   FOOD & DRINK

15 🔒 Map p92, F4

Jam-packed local shop full of Greek products: oil, wine, cheese, nuts, honey and yoghurt. Herbs hang in bunches; lentils fill sacks. (📞210 756 0055; Proklou 31, Pangrati; ⊘9am-3pm Mon, Tue & Sat, to 6pm Wed, Thu & Fri; 🚃2, 4, 11)

Explore

National Archaeological Museum & Exarhia

Near the National Archaeological Museum, bohemian Exarhia has an alternative culture and history that sets it apart from Athens' trendier districts. Although partly gentrified, the neighbourhood retains a youthful and unconventional identity, thanks to a resident population of students, anarchists, artists, actors, old lefties and intellectuals. Fantastic flights of omnipresent graffiti and occasional riot police highlight its revolutionary role.

The Sights in a Day

☀ The magnificent collections at the **National Archaeological Museum** (pictured, left; p100) could easily fill your whole day – wander its rooms examining priceless Greek art and artefacts. While you're there, zip alongside to the **Epigraphical Museum** (p107) for ancient inscribed tablets.

☀ Break for lunch at any of Exarhia's great restaurants, such as **Yiantes** (p107) for a rather genteel setting or **Rozalia** (p109) for taverna-style family fare. Then take a stroll to look at the most modern of arts: fantastical and pointedly messaged graffiti.

☾ After a solid rest, plan for a late night bar-hopping Exarhia's renowned drinking holes: **Alexandrino** (p109) for classic cocktails, **Tralala** (p109) for a bohemian scene and **Blue Fox** (p109) for retro style. Alternatively, settle in for a round of edgy live music at **An Club** (p111) and **Ginger Ale** (p109) or a late-night *rembetika* (Greek blues) session at **Kavouras** (p111) or **Boemissa** (p111).

For a local's day in Exarhia, see p104.

👁 Top Sights

National Archaeological Museum (p100)

🔍 Local Life

Neighbourhood Life in Exarhia (p104)

💜 Best of Athens

Food
Kimatothrafstis (p109)

Bars
Alexandrino (p109)

Blue Fox (p109)

Ginger Ale (p109)

Entertainment
AN Club (p111)

Kavouras (p111)

Getting There

Ⓜ **Metro** Omonia station (red and green lines) sits due west of Exarhia. Use Panepistimiou station (red line) for southern Exarhia. For the National Archaeological Museum, use Viktoria station (green line) and walk 10 minutes.

🚋 **Trolleybus** Also for the museum, catch trolleybus 2, 4, 5, 9 or 11 from outside St Denis Cathedral (Panepistimiou 24) and get off at the Polytechnio stop.

Top Sights
National Archaeological Museum

One of the world's most important museums, the National Archaeological Museum in Exarhia, houses the world's finest collection of Greek antiquities. Treasures offering a view of Greek art and history dating from the neolithic era to classical periods include exquisite sculptures, pottery, jewellery, frescoes and artefacts found throughout Greece. Allow plenty of time to view the vast and spectacular collections (more than 11,000 items) housed in this enormous 19th-century neoclassical building (8000 sq metres). The museum also hosts world-class temporary exhibitions.

Map p106, B1

213 214 4800

www.namuseum.gr

28 Oktovriou-Patision 44

adult/child €7/free

8am-8pm Apr-Oct, reduced hours Nov-Mar

M Viktoria, 2, 4, 5, 9 or 11 to Polytechnio

Don't Miss

Prehistoric Collection & Mycenaen Antiquities

Ahead of you as you enter the museum is the prehistoric collection, showcasing some of the most important pieces of Mycenaean, neolithic and Cycladic art, many in solid gold. The fabulous collection of Mycenaean antiquities (Gallery 4) is the museum's tour de force.

Mask of Agamemnon

The first cabinet holds the celebrated gold Mask of Agamemnon, unearthed at Mycenae by Heinrich Schliemann, along with key finds from Grave Circle A, including bronze daggers with intricate representations of the hunt.

Vaphio Cups

The exquisite Vaphio gold cups, with scenes of men taming wild bulls, are regarded to be among the finest surviving examples of Mycenaean art. They were found in a *tholos* (Mycenaean tomb shaped like a beehive) at Vaphio, near Sparta.

Cycladic Collection

The Cycladic collection in Gallery 6 includes the superb figurines of the 3rd and 2nd millennia BC that inspired artists such as Picasso. One splendid example measures 1.52m and dates from 2600 to 2300 BC.

Sounion Kouros

The galleries to the left of the entrance house the oldest and most significant pieces of the sculpture collection. Galleries 7 to 13 exhibit fine examples of Archaic *kouroi* (male statues) from the 7th century BC to 480 BC. The colossal 600 BC Sounion Kouros (Room 8), found at the Temple of Poseidon in Sounion, is made of Naxian marble and stood before Poseidon's temple.

☑ Top Tips

▶ Arrive early in the day or late in the evening to beat the rush.

▶ Allow plenty of time: with 8000 sq metres of exhibition space, it could take several visits to appreciate the museum's vast holdings, but it's possible to see the highlights in a half-day.

▶ Exhibits are displayed largely thematically. For more information get an audioguide.

✕ Take a Break

The museum cafe in the basement extends into an open-air internal courtyard. Or nip outside for coffee at **Brown BCB Bar** (☏210 383 9495; Tositsa 8, Exarhia; ◷9am-late; Ⓜ Viktoria), an airy cafe around the corner.

For a meal, the best bet is to head into Exarhia, to a place like Yiantes (p107) for fresh modern Greek food with a glass of wine.

National Archaeological Museum

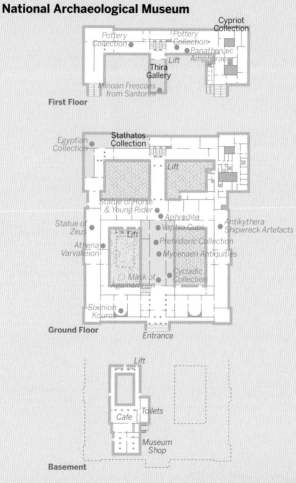

First Floor

Cypriot Collection

Pottery Collection

Pottery Collection

Panathenaic Amphorae

Lift

Thira Gallery

Minoan Frescoes from Santorini

Ground Floor

Egyptian Collection

Stathatos Collection

Lift

Statue of Horse & Young Rider

Aphrodite

Vaphio Cups

Antikythera Shipwreck Artefacts

Statue of Zeus

Lift

Prehistoric Collection

Athena Varvakeion

Mycenaen Antiquities

Mask of Agamemnon

Cycladic Collection

Sounion Kouros

Entrance

Basement

Lift

Cafe

Toilets

Museum Shop

Bronze God

Gallery 15 is dominated by the incredible 460 BC bronze statue of Zeus or Poseidon, found in the sea off Evia, which depicts one of the gods (no one really knows which) with his arms outstretched and holding a thunderbolt or trident in his right hand.

Athena Varvakeion

The 200-BC statue of Athena Varvakeion in Gallery 20 is the most famous copy – much reduced in size – of the colossal statue of Athena Polias by Pheidias that once stood in the Parthenon.

Horse & Rider

In Gallery 21 you will see the striking 2nd-century-BC statue of a horse and young rider, recovered from a shipwreck off Cape Artemision in Evia. Opposite the horse are several lesser-known but equally exquisite works such as the statue of Aphrodite, showing a demure nude Aphrodite struggling to hold her draped gown over herself.

Antikythera Shipwreck

Precious treasures discovered in 1900 by sponge divers off the island of Antikythera (Gallery 28) include the Antikythera Mechanism, an elaborate device for predicting astronomical positions, and the striking *Antikythera Youth* bronze statue.

Egyptian Gallery

The two-room (40 and 41) Egyptian gallery presents the best of the museum's significant collection, the only one in Greece. Dating from 5000 BC to the Roman conquest, artefacts include mummies, Fayum portraits and bronze figurines.

Minoan Frescoes

Upstairs, the spectacular Minoan frescoes from Santorini (Thira) were uncovered in the prehistoric settlement of Akrotiri, which was buried by a volcanic eruption in the late 16th century BC. The frescoes include *Boxing Children* and *Spring*, depicting red lilies and a pair of swallows kissing in midair. The Thira Gallery also has videos showing the 1926 eruption and the Akrotiri excavation.

Pottery Collection

The superb pottery collection traces the development of pottery from the Bronze Age through the Protogeometric and Geometric periods to the famous Attic black-figured pottery (6th century BC) and red-figured pottery (late 5th to early 4th centuries BC). Other uniquely Athenian vessels are the Attic White Lekythoi, slender vases depicting scenes at tombs.

Panathenaic Amphorae

In the centre of Gallery 56 are six Panathenaic amphorae, presented to the winners of the Panathenaic Games. Each amphora (vase-shaped ceramic vessel) contained oil from the sacred olive trees of Athens and victors might have received up to 140 of them. They are painted with scenes from the relevant sport (in this case wrestling) on one side and an armed Athena *promachos* (champion) on the other.

Local Life
Neighbourhood Life in Exarhia

Exarhia has an eclectic mix of comic stores, record shops, publishing houses, computer and alternative book and clothing stores. It has a vibrant bar scene, good-value eateries, and rock and *rembetika* (Greek blues) clubs. Plateia Exarhion (Exarhion Sq) is the neighbourhood's focal point, with many tavernas along pedestrian Valtestiou and Benaki, and bustling cafes and bars around nearly every corner.

❶ Plateia Exarhion

Plateia Exarhion is the epicentre of neighbourhood life. Pick a spot on the square for prime people-watching. Locals choose modern cafe-bookshop **Floral** (☎210 380 0070; www.floralcafe.gr; Themistokleous 80, Exarhia; ⊙9am-late; 🛜; Ⓜ Omonia), with grey-toned images of retro life and, you guessed it, flowers on the walls. Folks buy books, use the wi-fi, chat and watch the world go by.

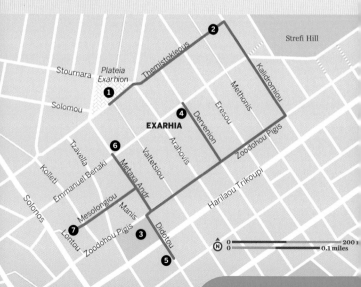

It's a good place to start the day or evening before exploring.

❷ Graffiti A-Go-Go

The walls, alleys and stairways of Exarhia are adorned with, possibly, some of the world's most creative graffiti. Often with a pointed underlying political message, these elaborate works are an inspiration to behold. Start at the Strefi Hill end of Themistokleous and simply wander the neighbourhood, looking for the latest expressions of both fancy and ire.

❸ Reclaimed Square

The inhabitants of Exarhia took back an entire city block, turning it into a completely locally planted and maintained urban park. See the reclaimed square bordered by Didotou, Harilaou Trikoupi, Navarinou and Zoodohou Pigis – a real work in progress.

❹ Old-World Taverna

Lunch at Exarhia institution **Barbagiannis** (☎210 330 0185; Emmanuel Benaki 94, Exarhia; mains €5-8; ⏰lunch & dinner; Ⓜ Omonia), an extremely low-key *mayirio* (cookhouse) on a quiet corner. Choose from the variety of big trays of traditional dishes behind the counter, such as *pastitsio* (layers of baked macaroni and minced meat), washed down with house wine.

❺ Records & Comics

Exarhia's fun music and comic-book shops include the chance to pick up, among other things, old-school vinyl and niche comics. Serious music fans comb **Spindle** (☎210 362 5362; www. spindlevinylrecords.gr; 49 Didotou, Exarhia; ⏰10am-6pm Mon, Wed & Sat, to 9pm Tue, Thu & Fri; Ⓜ Panepistimio) for eclectic indie, punk and rock new and used vinyl.

❻ Go Cretan for Dinner

Neighbourhood denizens love **Rakoumel** (☎210 380 0506; www.rakoumel. gr; Emmanuel Benaki 71, Exarhia; dishes €5-9; ⏰1pm-3am Mon-Sat; 📶; Ⓜ Omonia) and **Oxo Nou** (☎210 380 1778; Emmanuel Benaki 63-65, Exarhia; mains €8-11; ⏰3pm-late; 📶; Ⓜ Omonia) for their super Cretan food. These lively restaurants are just a block apart, so it's easy to browse both. Join homesick Cretans sipping *rakomelo* (honey-infused *raki* liquor) while sampling small plates featuring mountain herbs and slow-cooked meats.

❼ Live Local Music

Athenians come to Exarhia for its offbeat bars, live-music venues and *rembetika* clubs. Hop down to the bar strip at Mesolongiou to start your night, and see what happens.

National Archaeological Museum

Band playing *rembetika* (Greek blues; p110)

Sights

Epigraphical Museum   MUSEUM

1 ⊙ Map p106, B2

This 'library of stones' houses an important collection of Greek inscriptions detailing official records, including lists of war dead, tribute lists showing annual payments by Athens' allies, and the decree ordering the evacuation of Athens before the 480 BC Persian invasion. (☎210 821 7637; http://odysseus.culture.gr; Tositsa 1, Exarhia; admission free; ⊙8.30am-3pm Tue-Sun; Ⓜ Viktoria)

Eating

Yiantes   TAVERNA €€

2 ✕ Map p106, C3

This modern eatery, with its white linen and fresh-cut flowers set in a lovely garden courtyard, is upmarket for Exarhia, but the food is superb and made with largely organic produce. Try interesting greens such as *almirikia,* the perfectly grilled fish or delicious mussels and calamari with saffron. (☎210 330 1369; Valtetsiou 44, Exarhia; mains €9-12; ⊙1pm-midnight; ✈; Ⓜ Omonia)

Understand
Greece's Military Dictatorship

Coup & Repression

Exarhia's anarchic reputation has roots in its associations with radical politics and the infamous student sit-in at the neighbourhood's Athens Polytechnio (Technical University), under the junta. This military dictatorship was headed by a group of army colonels, led by Georgios Papadopoulos and Stylianos Patakos, which staged a coup on 21 April 1967. They established a military junta with Papadopoulos as prime minister. King Constantine tried an unsuccessful countercoup in December, after which he fled to Rome, then London.

The colonels declared martial law, banned political parties and trade unions, imposed censorship and imprisoned, tortured and exiled thousands of dissidents, including actress and activist Melina Mercouri. In June 1972 Papadopoulos declared Greece a republic and appointed himself president. On 17 November 1973, tanks stormed a building at the Athens Polytechnio to quell a student occupation calling for an uprising against the US-backed junta. While the number of casualties is still in dispute, the act was the death knell for the junta.

The Fall of the Junta

Shortly after, the head of the military security police, Dimitrios Ioannidis, deposed Papadopoulos. In July 1974 Ioannidis tried to impose unity with Cyprus by attempting to topple the Makarios government in Cyprus; Makarios got wind of an assassination attempt and escaped. The junta replaced him with the extremist Nikos Sampson as president. Consequently, mainland Turkey sent in troops until they occupied northern Cyprus, partitioning the country and displacing almost 200,000 Greek Cypriots who fled their homes for the safety of the south. The junta dictatorship collapsed.

Restoration of Democracy

Konstandinos Karamanlis was summoned from Paris to take office and his New Democracy (ND) party won a large majority at the November elections in 1974 against the newly formed Panhellenic Socialist Union (PASOK), led by Andreas Papandreou (son of Georgios Papandreou, prime minster of Greece from 2009 to 2011). A plebiscite voted 69% against the restoration of the monarchy and a ban on communist parties was lifted.

Kimatothrafstis

TAVERNA €

3 🍴 Map p106, D4

This great-value, bright and casual modern cafe with communal tables dishes out a range of home-style Greek cooking and alternative fare. Choose from the buffet of the day's offerings. Plates come in two sizes: big or small. (📞213 030 8274; Harilaou Trikoupi 49, Exarhia; small/large plates €3.80/6.80; ⏰8am-11pm, closed dinner Sun; 🛜; Ⓜ Omonia)

Rozalia

TAVERNA €

4 🍴 Map p106, C3

An Exarhia favourite on a lively pedestrian strip, this family-run taverna serves grills and home-style fare. (📞210 330 2933; www.rozalia.gr; Valtetsiou 58, Exarhia; mains €5-11; Ⓜ Omonia)

Drinking

Alexandrino

COCKTAIL BAR

5 🍸 Map p106, C3

This bar feels like a cute tiny French bistro, with excellent wines and cocktails. (📞210 382 7780; Emmanuel Benaki 69, Exarhia; ⏰7pm-late; Ⓜ Omonia)

Tralala

BAR

6 🍸 Map p106, D4

Actors frequent cool Tralala, with its original artwork, lively owners and gregarious atmosphere. (📞210 362 8066; Asklipiou 45, Exarhia; ⏰11pm-3am; Ⓜ Panepistimio, Omonia)

✅ Top Tip

Safety

While Exarhia is a mainstay residential neighbourhood, it has been known to be sketchy (petty thefts) at night. During times of political protest, it is best to steer clear. Keep informed and use your common sense.

Ginger Ale

CAFE, BAR

7 🍸 Map p106, C3

Dip back in time to a '50s veneered coffee shop–cum–rocking nightspot. Sip espresso by day and catch a rotating line-up of live acts by night. (📞210 330 1246; Themistokleous 74, Exarhia; ⏰8am-late; Ⓜ Omonia)

Blue Fox

BAR

8 🍸 Map p106, E3

You might not expect this in Athens, but Blue Fox is great for '50s-era swing and rockabilly, complete with Vespas and poodle skirts. (📞6942487225; Asklipiou 91, Exarhia; ⏰10pm-2am; Ⓜ Omonia)

Revolt

BAR

9 🍸 Map p106, B3

This small, simple bar with tables spilling out onto a pedestrianised square anchors a few solid blocks of good nightlife. The vibrant murals out front are super. Start here and explore. (📞210 380 0016; Kolleti 29, Exarhia; ⏰11am-2am; Ⓜ Omonia)

Local Life
Saturday Steet Market

Every Saturday morning locals make the trek up to the Kalidromiou, in the foothills of Strefi Hill, to Exarhia's weekly *laïki agora* (farmers market; ⏰6am-2pm Sat; 🚌026, Ⓜ Omonia), an enduring Athens institution. One of Athens' most atmospheric markets sees rowdy traders hawk fresh produce and household goods over one of Exarhia's finest streets. Get a prime seat at one of the busy cafes.

Circus
CAFE, COCKTAIL BAR

10 Ⓠ Map p106, C4

Presided over by a Ganesh-style wire elephant, Circus has relaxed coffees by day and cocktails by night. (☎210 361 5255; www.circusbar.gr; Navarinou 11, Exarhia; ⏰10am-late; 🛜; Ⓜ Panepistimiou)

Tsin Tsin
COCKTAIL BAR

11 Ⓠ Map p106, B4

Teeny, tiny and out of the way, but the bartender is a true mixologist, and the loungey feel is relaxing. (☎210 384 1460; Kiafas 6, Exarhia; ⏰7pm-late; Ⓜ Omonia)

Understand
Greek Music Scene

Athens has a thriving live-music scene in winter, when you can hear the gamut of Greek music, from the popular soulful Greek blues known as *rembetika* to traditional folk music, ethnic jazz, and even Greek rock, rap and hip hop. Athens' many intimate winter venues (most only operate between October and April) also host an eclectic range of touring indie rock, jazz and international artists. In summer live music is confined to festivals and out-door concerts by local artists and touring acts.

A unique part of Athenian nightlife are the *bouzoukia*, glitzy and expensive cabaret-style venues (often referred to as *skyladika* – dog houses – because of the crooning singers), where women dancing the sinewy *tsifteteli* (belly dance) are showered with expensive trays of carnations and revellers party until sunrise.

Popular Greek artists include consummate mainstream performers such as Haris Alexiou, Eleftheria Arvanitaki, George Dalaras, Dimitra Galani and Alkistis Protopsalti. Greece's big pop acts put on spectacular shows; look out for Anna Vissi, Antonis Remos, Despina Vandi, Notis Sfakianakis, Ploutarhos, Sakis Rouvas, Mihalis Hatziyiannis and Elena Paparizou.

Entertainment

AN Club
LIVE MUSIC

12 ⭐ Map p106, B3

A small spot for lesser-known international and local rock bands. (☎210 330 5056; www.anclub.gr; Solomou 13-15, Exarhia; Ⓜ Omonia)

Kavouras
TRADITIONAL MUSIC

13 ⭐ Map p106, C3

Above Exarhia's popular souvlaki joint, this lively club usually plays until dawn for a student crowd. (☎210 381 0202; Themistokleous 64, Exarhia; ⊙11pm-late Thu-Sat, closed Jul & Aug; Ⓜ Omonia)

Vox
CINEMA

14 ⭐ Map p106, C3

Vox open-air cinema on Exarhia's main square screens occasional movies. (☎210 331 0170; Themistokleous 82, Exarhia; Ⓜ Omonia)

Boemissa
TRADITIONAL MUSIC

15 ⭐ Map p106, B3

Rembetika, *laïka* (urban popular music) and decent grub are on offer at this divey joint. (☎210 383 8803; www.boemissa.gr; Solomou 13-15, Exarhia; ⊙10pm-late Thu-Sat; Ⓜ Omonia)

Shopping

Thymari tou Strefi
FOOD, WINE

16 🔒 Map p106, D2

Right in the thick of Saturday's lively street market, this quaint deli has a delectable array of traditional products, honey, cheese and regional specialities, as well as organic wine and ouzo. (☎210 330 0384; Kalidromiou 51a, Exarhia; ⊙9am-6pm Mon & Wed, 9am-9pm Tue, Thu & Fri, 8am-4pm Sat ; Ⓜ Omonia)

Comicon Shop
COMIC BOOKS

17 🔒 Map p106, C3

Browse a full range of Greek indie comics, graphic novels and fanzines. (☎213 008 0255; www.comicon-shop.gr; Solonos 128, Exarhia; Ⓜ Omonia)

Local Life
Rembetika

Join the dancing at one of Athens' longest-running *rembetika* (blues songs) haunts. **Rembetika Istoria** (☎210 642 4937; www.rebetikiistoria. com; Ippokratous 181, Exarhia - Neapolis; ⊙11pm-late Tue-Sun Oct-May; Ⓜ Omonia, Ambelokipi) has live music nightly with dinner or mezedhes and raucous good times into the wee hours.

Filopappou Hill & Thisio

Filopappou Hill (pictured, above), also known as the Hill of the Muses, offers the best eye-level views of the Acropolis from the top. The sedate Thisio neighbourhood, just to the north, blossomed after cars were banished to make way for the pedestrian promenade. Young Athenians have claimed the cafe precinct that emerged under the Acropolis, and the low-key residential streets make a nice change from the more heavily touristed centre.

The Sights in a Day

☀ Stroll **Filopappou Hill** (p114) in the morning, photographing the Acropolis, the Saronic Gulf and the mountains of the Attic basin. On its slopes explore ancient battlements, a shrine to the muses, Socrates' prison and a quiet Byzantine church.

☼ Then lunch in Thisio on traditional Greek fare at **Gevomai Kai Magevomai** (p119) and relax with a long coffee-drinking and people-watching session, as the locals do, on the cafe strips. Or stop in at **Peonia Herbs** (p121) for a special tea experience. When you're rejuvenated, take in a bit of modern art: **Herakleidon Museum** (p119) has work by Escher and Vasarely, while **Bernier-Eliades** (p119) shows high-profile contemporary art.

☾ Get tickets for **Dora Stratou Dance Theatre** (p121) to see an amazing array of Greek dances in elaborate costumes in an open-air theatre on Filopappou Hill, or watch a movie at the equally alfresco **Thission** (p121) – which has Acropolis views – then hit the bars.

◉ Top Sights
Filopappou Hill (p114)

♥ Best of Athens
Art Galleries
Bernier/Eliades (p119)

Entertainment
Dora Stratou Dance Theatre (p121)

Thission (p121)

Getting There

Ⓜ**Metro** To enter the Thisio neighbourhood directly, use the Thisio station (green line) and walk up pedestrianised Apostolou Pavlou. To reach Filopappou Hill, either walk through Thisio, or use the Akropoli station (red line) and walk west, past the Acropolis Museum, on either Rovertou Galli or pedestrianised Dionysiou Areopagitou.

Top Sights
Filopappou Hill

Also called the Hill of the Muses, Filopappou Hill – along with the Hills of the Pnyx and Nymphs – was, according to Plutarch, where Theseus and the Amazons did battle. Inhabited from prehistoric times to the post-Byzantine era, today the pine-clad slopes are a relaxing place for a stroll. They offer excellent views of Attica and the Saronic Gulf, and some of the very best vantage points for photographing the Acropolis. There are also some notable ruins.

👁 Map p116, C5

Ⓜ Akropoli

Monument of Filopappos

Don't Miss

Church of Agios Dimitrios Loumbardiaris

The 16th-century Church of Agios Dimitrios Loumbardiaris (Greek for cannon) is named after an incident in which a gunner from a Turkish garrison on the Acropolis was killed by a thunderbolt while attempting to fire a cannon on the Christian congregation. It has an old-world feel with a smell of incense, marble floors, a timber roof, and myriad icons and frescoes.

Socrates' Prison

Enter the cover of pines, with doves cooing, and follow the path to this warren of rooms carved into bedrock and rumoured to have been Socrates' prison. During WWII artefacts from the Acropolis and National Archaeological Museum were secreted here, sealed behind a wall.

Shrine of the Muses & Fortifications

Up the marble-cobbled stairs you'll reach a ruined shrine to the Muses, to whom this hill was deemed sacred. Even today grateful or hopeful artists place offerings on a small stone cairn. Also, ruins of 4th- and 5th-century-BC defensive walls criss-cross the hill.

Monument of Filopappos

The 12m Monument of Filopappos crowns the summit of the hill. Built between 114 and 116 AD in honour of Julius Antiochus Filopappos, a Roman consul and administrator, the monument's top middle niche depicted Filopappos enthroned, the bottom frieze showed him in a chariot with his entourage.

☑ Top Tips

▶ Small paths weave all over the hill, but the paved path to the top starts near the *periptero* (kiosk) on Dionysiou Areopagitou.

▶ Bring camera gear: the summit gives one of the best views of the Acropolis and Attica – sunset and evening offer spectacular light.

▶ The hill top above the treeline is exposed: bring sunscreen, a hat and water, rainwear on wet days.

▶ English-language placards placed at major features explain the rich ancient history of the hill.

✕ Take a Break

Visit Thisio's cafes or restaurants such as Filistron (p119) and Gevomai Kai Magevomai (p119).

Alternatively, lovely **Dionysos** (☏210 923 1936; www.dionysoszonars. gr; Rovertou Galli 43, Makrygianni; mains €19-36; ⏱restaurant noon-1am, cafe 8am-1am; Ⓜ Akropoli) offers drinks with views or a fine meal.

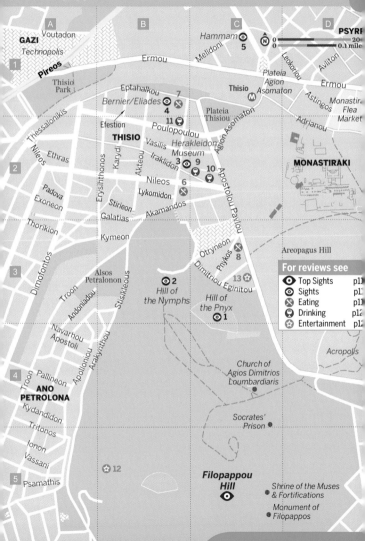

GAZI

Voutadon

Technopolis

Pireos

Thisio Park

Ermou

Melidoni

Hammam **5**

PSYRI

N 0   20
0   0.1 mile

Leokoriou

Aviiton

Ermou

Astingos

Monastir
Flea
Market

Plateia
Agion
Asomaton

Thisio **M**

Adrianou

Thessalonikis

Nileos

Ethras

Eptahalkou **7**

Bernier/Eliades **4**

Efestion

THISIO

Poulopoulou

Vasilis

Akteou

Karydi

Erysihthonos

Padova

Exoneon

Thorikion

Stirieon

Galatias

Kymeon

Dimofontos

Troon

Andoniadou

Alsos
Petralonon

Stisikleous

Navarhou
Apostoli

Apolloniou

Arakynthou

ANO
PETROLONA

Troon Pallineon

Kydandidon

Tritonos

Ionon

Vassani

Psamathis

Heralkleidon
Museum

Iraklidon

3 **9**

Nileos

Lykomidon

Akamandos

10

11

6

Plateia
Thisiou

Agion Asomaton

Apostoliou Pavlou

MONASTIRAKI

Otryneon

Pnykos **8**

Dimitriou Eginitou **13**

Areopagus Hill

Hill of
the Nymphs **2**

Hill of
the Pnyx **1**

Acropolis

Church of
Agios Dimitrios
Loumbardiaris

Socrates'
Prison

12

**Filopappou
Hill**
◉

Shrine of the Muses
& Fortifications

Monument of
Filopappos

GEORGE TSAFOS/GETTY IMAGES ©

MC Escher collection, Herakleidon Museum (p119)

Sights

Hill of the Pnyx   PARK

1 ⊙ Map p116, C3

North of Filopappou Hill, this rocky hill was the meeting place of the Democratic Assembly in the 5th century BC, where the great orators Aristides, Demosthenes, Pericles and Themistocles addressed assemblies. This less-visited site offers great views over Athens and a peaceful walk. (Ⓜ Thisio)

Hill of the Nymphs   PARK

2 ⊙ Map p116, B3

Northwest of Hill of the Pnyx, this hill is home to the old Athens observatory, built in 1842. (Ⓜ Thisio)

Q Local Life
Sunday Flea Market

A ragtag **Sunday flea market** (Ermou, Thisio; ☺dawn-2pm Sun; ⓂThisio, Keramikos) takes place on Ermou starting at the entrance to Keramikos and running towards Thisio Park and Gazi. It's not for everyone, with its jumble of often-ratty belongings. Traders peddle their motley cast-offs and discount wares, while bargain-hunters scour the aisles in search of that special something. This is the place to test your haggling skills.

Understand

Greek Gods

------- ------- ------- ------- ------- ------- -------

Ancient Greece revolved around the worship of 12 central gods and goddesses, all of which played a major role in the *mythos* (mythology). Each city-state had its own patron god or goddess, to be appeased and flattered, while on a personal level a farmer might make sacrifice to the goddess Demeter to bless his crops, or a fisherman to Poseidon to bring him fish and safe passage on the waves.

The Ancient Pantheon

Zeus (Jupiter) Heavyweight champ of Mt Olympus, lord of the skies and master of disguise in pursuit of mortal maidens.

Poseidon (Neptune) God of the seas, master of the mists and younger brother of Zeus.

Hera (Juno) Protector of women and family, the queen of heaven was also the embattled wife of Zeus.

Hades (Pluto) God of death, he ruled the underworld, bringing in newly dead with the help of his skeletal ferryman, Charon.

Athena (Minerva) Goddess of wisdom, war and science, and guardian of Athens.

Aphrodite (Venus) Goddess of love and beauty.

Apollo God of music, light, the arts and fortune-telling.

Artemis (Diana) The goddess of the hunt and twin sister of Apollo was, ironically, patron saint of wild animals.

Ares (Mars) God of war. Zeus' least favourite of his progeny.

Hermes (Mercury) Messenger of the gods, patron saint of travellers.

Hephaestus (Vulcan) God of craftsmanship, metallurgy and fire; he made the world's first woman of clay, Pandora, as a punishment for man.

Hestia (Vesta) Goddess of the hearth, she protected state fires in city halls where citizens of Greece could heat their brands.

Herakleidon Museum

MUSEUM

3 ⊙ Map p116, B2

This superb private museum showcases the interrelation of art, mathematics and philosophy. The permanent collection includes one of the world's biggest collections of MC Escher, as well as works from Victor Vasarely, in a beautifully restored neoclassical mansion. Extensive educational programs include excellent two-hour guided tour-seminars in English, available with advance booking (€25, minimum of 10 participants required). (☎210 346 1981; www.herakleidon-art.gr; Herakleidon 16, Thisio; adult/child €6/free; ⊙10am-6pm Sun Jun, Jul, Sep & Oct; ⓜThisio)

Bernier/Eliades

GALLERY

4 ⊙ Map p116, B1

This well-established gallery showcases prominent Greek artists and an impressive list of international artists, from abstract American impressionists to British pop. (☎210 341 3935; www.bernier-eliades.gr; Eptachalkou 11, Thisio; ⊙10.30am-6.30pm Tue-Fri, noon-4pm Sat; ⓜThisio)

Hammam

SPA

5 ⊙ Map p116, C1

This little spa combines classic marble basins with modern amenities. It offers the full range of services from a basic *hammam* (Turkish bath; €25) to a host of massages and treatments. (☎210 323 1073; www.hammam.gr; Agion Asomaton 17

& Melidoni 1, Thisio; ⊙12.30-10pm Mon-Fri, 10am-10pm Sat & Sun; ⓜThisio)

Eating

Gevomai Kai Magevomai

TAVERNA €

6 ✕ Map p116, B2

Stroll off the pedestrian way to find this small corner taverna with marble-topped tables. Neighbourhood denizens know it as one of the best for home-cooked, simple food with the freshest ingredients. Menu changes constantly. (☎210 345 2802; Nileos 11, Thisio; mains €6-11; ⊙lunch & dinner; ⓐ; ⓜThisio)

To Steki tou Ilia

TAVERNA €

7 ✕ Map p116, B1

You'll often see people waiting for a table at this *psistaria* (restaurant serving grilled food), famous for its tasty grilled lamb and pork chops. With tables under the trees on the quiet pedestrian strip opposite the church, it's a no-frills place with barrel wine and simple dips, chips and salads. (☎210 345 8052; Eptahalkou 5, Thisio; chops per portion/kg €9/30; ⊙8pm-late; ⓜThisio)

Filistron

MEZEDHES €€

8 ✕ Map p116, C3

It's wise to book a prized table on the rooftop terrace of this *mezedhopoleio* (restaurant specialising in mezedhes) that enjoys breathtaking Acropolis and

Understand
Early Greek Philosophers

Late 5th- and early-4th-century-BC philosophers Aristotle, Plato and Socrates introduced new ways of thinking rooted not in the mysticism of myths, but rather in rationality, with a focus on logic and reason. Athens' greatest citizen, Socrates (469–399 BC), was forced to drink hemlock for his disbelief in the old gods, but before he died he bequeathed a school of hypothetical reductionism that is still used today. Plato (427–347 BC), his star student, was responsible for documenting his teacher's thoughts for posterity. Considered an idealist, he wrote *The Republic* as a warning to the city-state of Athens that unless its people respected law, leadership and educated its youth sufficiently, it would be doomed. His student Aristotle (384–322 BC), at the end of the Golden Age, was the personal physician to Philip II, king of Macedon, and the tutor of Alexander the Great, and focused his gifts on astronomy, physics, zoology, ethics and politics. The greatest gift of the Athenian philosophers to modern-day thought is their spirit of rational inquiry.

Lykavittos views. It has a large range of decent mezedhes and an extensive Greek wine list, though service sometimes suffers. (☏210 346 7554; Apostolou Pavlou 23, Thisio; mezedhes €8-14; ☺6pm-midnight Tue-Sun; Ⓜ Thisio)

Drinking

Root Artspace   CAFE
9 Ⓜ Map p116, C2

Cafe meets bar meets live-music and art venue in a renovated 19th-century stone stable, Root Artspace makes for a good hang-out in the shadow of the Acropolis. Check online for art and entertainment line-up. (☏210 345 0003; www.rootartspace.gr; Iraklidon 10, Thisio; ☺9am-1am; Ⓜ Thisio)

Sin Athina   CAFE
10 Ⓜ Map p116, C2

Location, location, location! This little cafe-bar sits at the junction of the two pedestrianised cafe strips, and has a sweeping view up to the Acropolis. (☏210 345 5550; www.sinathina.gr; Iraklidon 2, Thisio; ☺8am-late; Ⓜ Thisio)

☑ Top Tip
Drinking in Thisio

Cafes along Thisio's pedestrian promenade Apostolou Pavlou have great Acropolis views. The string of cafes and bars along pedestrianised Iraklidon also draws 'em in. So just wander and see what appeals.

Cafes along Iraklidon St, Thisio

Peonia Herbs TEAHOUSE

11 🕴 Map p116, B2

There's an instantly calming, smoke-free aura to this herb shop and tearoom. (☏210 341 0260; www.peonia.gr; Amfiktyonos 12, Thisio; ⏱10am-4pm Mon-Fri, to 3pm Sat; MThisio)

Entertainment

Dora Stratou Dance Theatre DANCE

12 ⭐ Map p116, B5

Every summer this company performs its repertoire of Greek folk dances at its open-air theatre on the western side of Filopappou Hill. It also runs folk-dancing workshops in summer. (☏210 324 4395; www.grdance.org; Filopappou Hill; adult/child €15/5; ⏱performances 9.30pm Wed-Fri, 8.15pm Sat & Sun Jun-Sep; MPetralona, Akropoli)

Thission CINEMA

13 ⭐ Map p116, C3

Across from the Acropolis, this is a lovely old-style cinema in a garden setting. Sit towards the back if you want to catch a glimpse of the glowing edifice. (☏210 342 0864; www.cine-thisio.gr; Apostolou Pavlou 7, Thisio; MThisio)

Explore

Keramikos & Gazi

Like a beacon, the illuminated red chimneys of the old Athens gasworks (Technopolis) lead you to Gazi, one of the city's best nightlife districts. Cool restaurants, bars and nightclubs alternate with museums, theatres and art spaces. If you go by foot from Thisio via pedestrianised Ermou, you pass Keramikos, the archaeological site of the city's ancient cemetery (pictured, above) and home of an excellent museum.

The Sights in a Day

☀ Begin at **Keramikos** (p124) and explore the extensive grounds and elaborate monuments early in the day – before it gets too hot. Then pop into its museum for superior sculptural artefacts. The nearby **Museum of Islamic Art** (p129) is the showcase of an extensive, exquisite collection and is well worth a visit.

☀ Take a break for lunch in Gazi at any number of fine eateries, such as **Kanella** (p130), a contemporary taverna with tasty basics. Then head down to the modern-art museum, **Benaki Museum Pireos Annexe** (p129), for top exhibitions, and wrap up with a coffee in its spacious cafe.

☾ Be sure to take a long nap so you can be out all night. For dinner, head to Gazi for one of the tavernas near the square, or Keramikos for fun **Athiri** (p130) with its verdant courtyard. When you're ready, the bar crawl begins... Start at **Hoxton** (p131) and see what happens.

For a local's night out in Keramikos and Gazi, see p126.

◉ Top Sights
Keramikos (p124)

◯ Local Life
A Night Out in Keramikos & Gazi (p126)

♥ Best of Athens

Museums
Museum of Islamic Art (p129)

Benaki Museum Pireos Annex (p129)

Food
Funky Gourmet (p126)

Aleria (p127)

Kanella (p130)

Bars
Gazarte (p127)

Hoxton (p131)

MoMix (p127)

Bios (p127)

Getting There

Ⓜ **Metro** Keramikos station (blue line) pops up in the centre of the Gazi neighbourhood. Parking is atrocious, so certainly use the metro. To reach the Keramikos archaeological site, Thisio station (green line) is a hair closer... just walk up Ermou to the site entrance.

Top Sights
Keramikos

A cemetery from 3000 BC to the 6th century AD (Roman times), Keramikos was originally a settlement for potters who were attracted by the clay on the banks of the River Iridanos. Because of frequent flooding, the area was ultimately converted into the city's primary cemetery, and now lies below street level due to silt deposits. Rediscovered by a worker in 1861 during the construction of Pireos street, Keramikos is now a lush, tranquil site with a fine museum and a collection of magnificent sculptures.

◉ Map p128, D2

☎ 210 346 3552

http://odysseus.culture.gr

Ermou 148, Keramikos

adult/child incl museum €2/free, with Acropolis pass free

⊙ 8am-8pm, reduced hours in low season

Ⓜ Thisio

Don't Miss

The Grounds
Once inside you'll find a plan of the site. A path leads down to the right to the remains of the city wall built by Themistocles in 479 BC, and rebuilt by Konon in 394 BC, and around the grounds. The wall is broken by the foundations of two gates; tiny signs mark each one.

Sacred Gate
The Sacred Gate spanned the Sacred Way, along which pilgrims from Eleusis entered the city during the annual Eleusian procession. Between the Sacred and Dipylon Gates are the foundations of the Pompeion, used as an important ceremonial centre for the Panathenaic Procession (p43).

Dipylon Gate
The once-massive Dipylon Gate was the city's main entrance and where the Panathenaic Procession began. It was also where the city's prostitutes gathered to offer their services to travellers. From a platform nearby, Pericles gave his famous speech extolling the virtues of Athens.

Street of Tombs
This avenue was reserved for the tombs of Athens' most prominent citizens. Some surviving *stelae* (grave slabs) are now in the on-site museum and the National Archaeological Museum; what you see are mostly replicas.

Archaeological Museum of Keramikos
The small but excellent museum contains remarkable *stelae* and sculptures from the site, such as the amazing 4th-century-BC marble bull from the plot of Dionysos of Kollytos, as well as funerary offerings and ancient toys.

☑ Top Tips

▶ Do not skip the museum – it contains superb original sculptures (reproductions were placed among the tombs when the sculptures were moved indoors for their protection).

▶ Bring your imagination: though many of the ceremonial buildings and gates no longer exist, this was a monumental gateway to the city for the ancients.

▶ Also bring water as there is no cafe or shop really nearby.

▶ Admission to the site and the museum is included in the Acropolis ticket.

✖ Take a Break

Either head to the cafes in Gazi for a sandwich or drink, or head towards the city centre on Ermou to the Thisio and Monastiraki neighbourhoods.

Local Life
A Night Out in Keramikos & Gazi

The towering pylons of Gazi's Technopolis are illuminated red at night, calling all partygoers. The maze of streets emanating away from Gazi's central *plateia* (square) and on into Keramikos are chock-a-block with restaurants and bars. While the line-up is ever-changing, we'll take you on a tour of some of the area's current top spots.

❶ Gastronomic Temple

Noveau gastronomy meets fresh Mediterranean ingredients at **Funky Gourmet** (✆210 524 2727; www.funky gourmet.com; Paramithias 3, cnr Salaminas, Keramikos; set menus from €80; ⊙7.30pm-1am Tue-Sat, last order 10.30pm; Ⓜ Metaxourgio), which earned a second Michelin star in 2015. Elegant lighting, refinement and sheer joy in food make this a worthwhile stop for any foodie. The degustation menus can

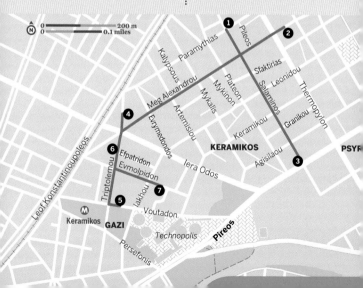

be paired with wines. Book ahead to get in.

❷ Dining Alfresco

Another fab date-night option, contemporary, elegant **Aleria** (📞210 522 2633; www.aleria.gr; Megalou Alexandrou 57, Metaxourghio; mains €12-20; ⊙8pm-midnight Mon-Sat, closed late Aug; Ⓜ Metaxourghio) is popular for its beautifully prepared local ingredients and its refined setting in a restored mansion. The softly lit courtyard is particularly inviting.

❸ Edgy Athens

In an industrial Bauhaus building near Gazi, the avant-garde multilevel warren called **Bios** (📞210 342 5335; www.bios.gr; Pireos 84, Gazi; ⊙11am-late; Ⓜ Thisio) has a bar, live performances, art and new-media exhibitions, a basement club, a tiny art-house cinema and a roof garden. It's a good stop if you're looking for the edgier side of Athens.

❹ Molecular Mixology

Athens' first molecular mixology bar, **MoMix** (📞6974350179; www.momix.gr; Keleou 1, Gazi; ⊙7pm-late; Ⓜ Keramikos) is the place to stop while you're in the mood to savour your cocktails. Get experimental with everything from a passionfruit mojito to the Amnesia Molecular Ice Cream, which resembles a kids' dessert (but with a vodka twist)!

❺ Heating It Up, with a View

In summer don't judge the action at ground level, head to the rooftop terraces. You'll find one of the best at **Gazarte** (📞210 346 0347; www.gazarte. gr; Voutadon 32-34, Gazi; Ⓜ Keramikos), where a cinema-sized video screen is dwarfed by the amazing city views taking in the Acropolis. Mainstream music and occasional live acts please a trendy 30-something crowd. It also has a cinema proper and a restaurant to boot.

❻ Gay Gazi

Gazi has quietly acquired one of Athens' best gay and lesbian scenes, with a gay triangle emerging near the railway line on Leoforos Konstantinoupoleos and Megalou Alexandrou. Tiny, sleek **Sodade** (📞210 346 8657; Triptolemou 10, Gazi; ⊙11pm-6am; Ⓜ Keramikos) is superfun for dancing. Nearby, Athens' main lesbian club, **Noiz** (📞210 346 7850; www.facebook.com/noizclubgaz; Konstantinoupoleos 78, Gazi; Ⓜ Keramikos), has retro dance nights.

❼ Hit a Club

Once you've laid on a few drinks, hit a club like **Pixi** (📞210 342 3751; www. pixi.gr; Evmolpidon 11, Gazi; Ⓜ Keramikos), where you'll find good DJs and flashing lights. Pixi's operators also throw summer parties at beach clubs on the Apollo Coast. You can cab it there if you're feeling flush!

METAXOURGIO

PSYRRI

Museum of Islamic Art ◉ 1

Museum of Traditional Pottery ◉ 4

KERAMIKOS

Keramikos ◉

THISIO

Plateia Thisiou

GAZI

Technopolis ◉ 3

Thisio Park

VOTANIKOS

ROUF

Benaki Museum 2 ◉ Pireos Annexe

Votanikos Kipos

200 m
0.1 miles

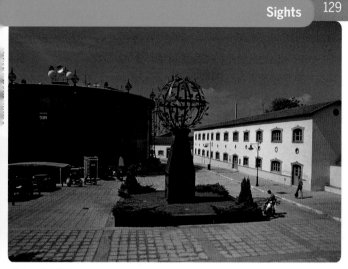

Technopolis (p130)

Sights

Museum of Islamic Art   MUSEUM

1 Map p128, E2

This museum showcases one of the world's most significant collections of Islamic art. Housed in two restored neoclassical mansions near Keramikos, it exhibits more than 8000 items representing the 12th to 19th centuries, including weavings, carvings, prayer rugs, tiles and ceramics. On the 3rd floor is a 17th-century reception room with an inlaid marble floor from a Cairo mansion. You can see part of the Themistoklean wall in the basement. (☏210 325 1311; www.benaki.gr; Agion Asomaton 22 & Dipylou 12, Keramikos; adult/child €7/free, Thu free; ⏱9am-5pm Thu-Sun; Ⓜ Thisio)

Benaki Museum Pireos Annexe   MUSEUM

2 Map p128, A4

This massive Pireos annex of the fine Benaki Museum (p76) is housed in a former industrial building and hosts contemporary visual arts, cultural and historical exhibitions, major international shows, and musical performances in the courtyard. It has an airy cafe and excellent gift shop. (☏210 345 3111; www.benaki.gr; Pireos 138, cnr Andronikou, Rouf; admission €4-6; ⏱10am-6pm Thu & Sun, to 10pm Fri & Sat, closed Aug; 🛈; Ⓜ Keramikos)

Technopolis
BUILDING

3 ⊙ Map p128, C3

There's always something on at the city's old gasworks, the impressively restored 1862 complex of furnaces and industrial buildings. It hosts multi-media exhibitions, concerts, festivals and special events and has a pleasant cafe. (☎210 346 7322; Pireos 100, Gazi; Ⓜ Keramikos)

Museum of Traditional Pottery
MUSEUM

4 ⊙ Map p128, E2

This small museum in a lovely neo-classical building around the corner from the Keramikos site is dedicated to the history of (relatively) contem-porary Greek pottery, exhibiting a selection from the museum's 4500-plus collection. There's a reconstruction of a traditional potter's workshop. The cen-tre holds periodic exhibitions. (☎210 331 8491; www.potterymuseum.gr; Melidoni 4-6, Keramikos; adult/child €3/free; ⊙9am-3pm Mon-Fri, closed Aug; Ⓜ Thisio)

> ☑ Top Tip
>
> ### Gazi Transport
>
> To get to Gazi, definitely take the metro to Keramikos station (or take a cab), which puts you smack in the middle of the scene, and cab it home in the wee hours.

Eating

Athiri
MODERN GREEK €€

5 🍴 Map p128, D2

Athiri's lovely garden courtyard is a verdant surprise in this pocket of Kera-mikos. The small but innovative menu plays on Greek regional classics. Try Santorini fava and the hearty beef stew with *myzithra* (sheep's-milk cheese) and handmade pasta from Karpathos. (☎210 346 2983; www.athirirestaurant.gr; Plateon 15, Keramikos; mains €12-19; ⊙8pm-1am Tue-Sat, 6pm-midnight Sun; Ⓜ Thisio)

Skoufias
TAVERNA €

6 🍴 Map p128, A4

This gem of a winter-only taverna near the railway line is a little off the beaten track but is worth seeking out. The menu has Cretan influences and an eclectic selection of regional Greek cuisine, including dishes you won't find in any tourist joint, from superb rooster with ouzo to lamb *tsigariasto* (braised) with *horta* (wild greens), and potato salad with orange. Dine outside at tables opposite a church. (☎210 341 2252; Vasiliou tou Megalou 50, Rouf; mains €5-9; ⊙9pm-late Oct-May; Ⓜ Keramikos)

Kanella
TAVERNA €

7 🍴 Map p128, B2

Homemade village-style bread, mis-matched retro crockery and brown-paper tablecloths set the

Understand
Menu Advice

Menus with prices must be displayed outside restaurants. English menus are fairly standard but off the beaten track you may encounter Greek-only menus. Many places display big trays of the day's *mayirefta* (ready-cooked meals) or encourage you to see what's cooking in the kitchen. Bread and occasionally small dips or nibbles are served on arrival (you're not given a choice, and it's added to the bill). Don't stick to the three-course paradigm – locals often share a range of starters and mains (or starters can be the whole meal). Dishes may arrive in no particular order. Frozen ingredients, especially seafood, are usually flagged on the menu (an asterisk or 'kat' on Greek menu). Fish is usually sold per kilogram rather than per portion, and is generally cooked whole rather than filleted. It is customary to go into the kitchen to select your fish (go for firm flesh and glistening eyes). Check the weight (raw) so there are no surprises on the bill.

tone for this trendy, modern taverna serving regional Greek cuisine. Friendly staff serve daily specials such as lemon lamb with potatoes, along with an excellent zucchini and avocado salad. (☏210 347 6320; www.kanellagazi.gr; Leoforos Konstantinoupoleos 70, Gazi; dishes €7-11; ☺1.30pm-late; Ⓜ Keramikos)

Oina Perdamata
TAVERNA €

8 ✗ Map p128, B3

Unpretentious, fresh daily specials are the hallmark of this simple spot just off busy Pireos. Try staples such as fried cod with garlic dip and roast vegetables, or pork stew, rabbit and rooster. (☏210 341 1461; www.oinomperdemata.gr; Vasiliou tou Megalou 10, Gazi; mains €5-10; ☺lunch & dinner; 🛜; Ⓜ Keramikos)

Sardelles
SEAFOOD €€

9 ✗ Map p128, C3

Dig into simply cooked seafood mezedhes at tables outside, opposite the illuminated gasworks. Nice touches include fishmonger paper tablecloths and souvenir pots of basil. Meat eaters can venture next door to its counterpart, **Butcher Shop** (☏210 341 3440; Persefonis 19, Gazi; ☺7-11.30pm; Ⓜ Keramikos). (☏210 347 8050; Persefonis 15, Gazi; fish dishes €10-17; ☺lunch & dinner; Ⓜ Keramikos)

Drinking

Hoxton
BAR

10 🍷 Map p128, B2

Join the hip, artsy crowd for shoulder-to-shoulder hobnobbing amid original art, iron beams and leather sofas. (☎210 341 3395; Voutadon 42, Gazi; ⊙1pm-late; Ⓜ Keramikos)

Gazaki   BAR

| 11 🚇 Map p128, B3 |

This Gazi trailblazer opened before the neighbourhood became *the* place to be. Friendly locals crowd the great rooftop bar. (☎6940629755; Triptolemou 31, Gazi; ⊙7pm-late; Ⓜ Keramikos)

45 Moires   BAR

| 12 🚇 Map p128, C2 |

Go deep into hard rock and enjoy terrace views of Gazi's neon-lit chimneys and the Acropolis. (☎210 347 2729; www.45moires.gr; Iakhou 18, cnr Voutadon, Gazi; Ⓜ Keramikos)

Nixon Bar   BAR

| 13 🚇 Map p128, D2 |

More chic than most, Nixon Bar serves up food and cocktails. (www.nixon.gr; Agisilaou 61b, Keramikos; ⊙7pm-late; Ⓜ Thisio)

S-Cape   GAY & LESBIAN

| 14 🚇 Map p128, C3 |

Stays packed with the younger gay, lesbian and transgender crowd. Check theme nights online. (www.s-capeclub.gr; Iakhou 32, Gazi; Ⓜ Keramikos)

Moe Club   GAY

| 15 🚇 Map p128, C1 |

After-hours hang-out with occasional special parties. (www.moeclub-gazi.

Ⓠ Local Life
Athens' Gay Nightlife

For the most part, Athens' gay and lesbian scene is relatively low-key, though the **Athens Pride** (www.athenspride.eu) march, held in June, has been an annual event since 2005. Check out www.athensinfoguide.com or a copy of the *Greek Gay Guide* booklet at *periptera* (newspaper kiosks).

For nightlife, Gazi has become Athens' gay and lesbian hub, with a gay triangle emerging near the railway line on Leoforos Konstantinoupoleos and Megalou Alexandrou. Gay and gay-friendly clubs around town are also found in Makrygianni, Psyrri, Metaxourgio and Exarhia.

blogspot.com; Keleou 5, Gazi; ⊙1am-6am; Ⓜ Keramikos)

A Liar Man   BAR

| 16 🚇 Map p128, B2 |

A tiny hideout with a more hushed vibe. It closes during summer. (☎210 342 6322; www.aliarman.gr; Sofroniou 2, Gazi; ⊙mid-Sep–mid-Jun; Ⓜ Keramikos)

BIG   GAY

| 17 🚇 Map p128, B1 |

Hub of Athens' lively bear scene. (☎6946282845; www.barbig.gr; Falesias 12, Gazi; ⊙10pm-4am Tue-Sun; Ⓜ Keramikos)

Museum of Traditional Pottery (p130)

Entertainment

Greek Film Archive
CINEMA

18 ⭐ Map p128, C1

Check the website for special film series. (Tainiothiki tis Ellados; 📞210 360 9695; www.tainiothiki.gr; Iera Odos 48, Gazi; Ⓜ Keramikos)

Fuzz
LIVE MUSIC

19 ⭐ Map p128, A4

Fuzz jams with international acts such as the Wailers and Gypsy punk band

Gogol Bordello. (📞210 345 0817; www. fuzzclub.gr; Pireos 209, Tavros; Ⓜ Petraluna)

Shopping

Rien
CLOTHING, ACCESSORIES

20 🔒 Map p128, C1

Penny Vomva designs stylish, sexy clothes with naturalistic lines. Her handbags are supple, colourful leather fancies. She also has a new boutique in Kolonaki. (📞210 342 0622; www.rien. gr; Triptolemou 2-4, Gazi; ⏰4-8pm Wed-Sat, or by appointment; Ⓜ Keramikos)

The Best of
Athens

Plateia Monastirakiou (Monastiraki Sq; p44)
MILAN GONDA/SHUTTERSTOCK ©

Best Walks
Ancient Athens

🏃 The Walk

The key ancient sites of Athens make for an action-packed but manageable walk, from the Temple of Olympian Zeus, past the Acropolis Museum and up to the Acropolis, then down around the other side of the hallowed hill into the Plaka and Monastiraki neighbourhoods, where you will find the Ancient Agora and Roman Agora. If you only have one day to see the sights, this is the walk to take.

Start Temple of Olympian Zeus; Ⓜ Akropoli

Finish Roman Agora; Ⓜ Monastiraki

Length 2.4km; three hours

🍴 Take a Break

Two of the easiest spots to stop for a bite to eat are the Acropolis Museum's cafe-restaurant (p31), with its magical views of the Parthenon, and **Kuzina** (📞 210 324 0133; www.kuzina.gr; Adrianou 9, Monastiraki; mains €12-25; 🕐 11am-late; Ⓜ Thisio), among the many good options on Adrianou, near the Ancient Agora, for contemporary creative Greek cuisine.

Odeon of Herodes Atticus (p28)

Y. DRAGON/GETTY IMAGES ©

❶ Temple of Olympian Zeus

The striking **Temple of Olympian Zeus** (p90), the largest temple in Greece, had 104 Corinthian columns, of which 15 remain. It was dedicated to supreme god Zeus. Peisistratos began building it in the 6th century BC, a succession of leaders continued, and Hadrian finally completed it in AD 131.

❷ Hadrian's Arch

Heading towards Plaka, teetering on the edge of the traffic, is **Hadrian's Arch** (p91), the ornate gateway erected in AD 132 to mark the boundary between Hadrian's Athens and the ancient city.

❸ Acropolis Museum

The landmark **Acropolis Museum** (p30) contains the precious sculptures from the Acropolis, preserved in spacious, well-lit glory. These include the Caryatids and amazing works from the Parthenon's pediments, metopes and frieze.

❹ Ancient Theatres

On the way up the southern slope of the Acropolis, explore the **Theatre of Dionysos** (p28), the birthplace of theatre, and the magnificent **Odeon of Herodes Atticus** (p28), built in AD 161 and still in use today.

❺ Acropolis

The **Acropolis** (p24) is the most important ancient site in the Western world. Take in its diminutive, restored Temple of Athena Nike,

then enter through the grand gates of the Propylaia to visit the iconic Parthenon as well as the Erechtheion, with its statuesque Porch of the Caryatids. On a clear day you can see for kilometres from the sweeping hill top.

❻ Ancient Agora

Exit the Acropolis from the north gate and visit ancient Athens' civic centre: the **Ancient Agora** (p40). The seat of democracy, philosophy and commerce, this rambling site, with the superb Temple of

Hephaestus, also has a top-notch museum in the colonnaded Stoa of Attalos.

❼ Roman Agora

The highlight of the **Roman Agora** (p48) is the well-preserved **Tower of the Winds** (p48). Built in the 1st century BC, it functioned as an ingenious sundial, weathervane, water clock and compass. Each side represents a point of the compass, and has a relief of a figure depicting the wind associated with that point.

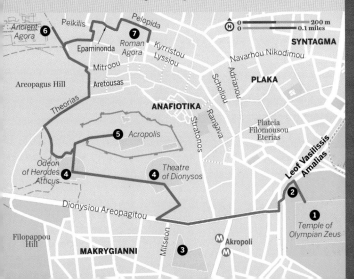

Best Walks
Syntagma & Plaka to Monastiraki

🏃 The Walk

Boisterous, monument-packed central Athens is best explored on foot. The historic centre, main archaeological sites, major landmarks, museums and attractions are close to one another. The main civic hub of Athens, Plateia Syntagmatos (Syntagma Sq) , merges into the historic Plaka and |Monastiraki neighbourhoods, which mesh one into the next, and make for a super stroll in which to soak up a bit of city-centre life. At any point along the way, ancient sites lie nearby, calling for a detour.

Start Plateia Syntagmatos; Ⓜ Syntagma

Finish Monastiraki Flea Market; Ⓜ Monastiraki

Length 2.5km; three hours

✕ Take a Break

Midway along the walk you can chill out at **Klepsydra** (📞 210 321 2493; Klepsydras & Thrasyvoulou, Plaka; snacks €4; 🕘 9am-1am; Ⓜ Monastiraki) cafe, which offers a quiet respite in the busy downtown.

GEORGE TSAFOS/GETTY IMAGES ©

Monastiraki Flea Market (p45)

❶ Plateia Syntagmatos

Start in this **square** (p64) named for the constitution granted on 3 September 1843. Time your visit to catch the **changing of the guard** (p64) outside the parliament building, every hour on the hour. To the left of the metro entrance spot a section of the ancient cemetery and the Peisistratos aqueduct.

❷ Lysikrates Monument

Built in 334 BC, the **Lysikrates Monument** (cnr Sellei & Lysikratous) stands in what was once part of the Street of Tripods (modern Tripodon), where winners of ancient dramatic and choral contests dedicated their tripod trophies to Dionysos. Reliefs depict the battle between Dionysos and the Tyrrhenian pirates, whom the god had transformed into dolphins.

❸ Anafiotika Quarter

On Stratonos, which skirts the Acropolis, rises the **Church of St George of the Rock**, which marks the entry to the Anafiotika quarter. This picturesque maze of little whitewashed houses is the legacy of stonemasons from the small Cycladic island of Anafi, who were brought in to build the king's palace after Independence.

4 Turkish Baths

Find the **Bath House of the Winds** (p50) on Kyrristou or other Turkish baths inside the free **Museum of Greek Popular Instruments** (p66), which has one of

Athens' only remaining private *hammams* in its gift shop.

5 Plateia Mitropoleos

Jaunt north to expansive **Plateia Mitropoleos**, with **Athens Cathedral** (p48) and its smaller, more historically significant neighbour: 12th-century Church of Agios Eleftherios, known as the Little Metropolis.

6 Hadrian's Library

Pandrosou, a relic of the old Turkish bazaar, is

full of souvenir shops and leads to **Hadrian's Library** (p50), once the most luxurious public building in the city, erected by the eponymous emperor around AD 132.

7 Monastiraki Flea Market

Wrap up with a wander in Monastiraki. The colourful, chaotic central square teems with street vendors and leads to shopper's or people-watcher's paradise: the **Monastiraki Flea Market** (p45).

Best Archaeological Sites

LONELY PLANET/GETTY IMAGES ©

A walk around the archaeological park that is Athens takes in highlights spread over millennia: from the neolithic period to the Classical, Roman and Byzantine eras. In addition to the human-made monuments discussed here, it's worth strolling the promenade up to Filopappou Hill and the Hill of the Pnyx to see ancient terrain and views of the city centre and its shining Acropolis.

Classical Age

The Classical Age (5th to 4th centuries BC) represents the apex in Greek building. Marble temples (characterised by the famous orders of columns: Doric, Ionic and Corinthian) are epitomised by the mother of all Doric structures, the 5th-century-BC Parthenon. The Greek theatre is also a hallmark of the classical period. The theatre's cleverly engineered acoustics meant every spectator could hear every word uttered on the stage below.

Roman Athens

The Romans used many of the Greek sites, such as the Panathenaic Stadium, adapting them to their needs and occasionally modifying them, or even completing them, as Hadrian did with Temple of Olympian Zeus.

Byzantine & Ottoman Athens

Church-building was particularly expressive during the Byzantine era in Greece (from around AD 700) and many churches remain, unlike the remarkably few monuments from the four centuries of Ottoman Turkish rule (16th to 19th centuries). Examples of the latter include parts of Plaka, its Fethiye Mosque and the Turkish Baths.

☑ Top Tips

▶ Due to financial difficulties, at the time of writing many sites operated on shorter winter hours (closing around 3pm). This may change.

▶ Be prepared with seasonal gear: sunscreen, hats and water in summer, rain gear in winter.

▶ Bring ID to qualify for student, senior citizen or EU discounts.

Mosaic, Church of Kapnikarea (p48)

Ancient Greek Sites

Acropolis The star of the show, towering over Athens and thrilling to behold. (p24)

Theatre of Dionysos The birthplace of theatre, on the Acropolis' southern slopes. (p28)

Ancient Agora Athens' civic, political and commercial centre in ancient times, beautifully preserved. (p40)

Keramikos The potters' quarter turned cemetery, and ceremonial entrance to Athens. (p124)

Temple of Olympian Zeus Greece's largest temple, it took over 700 years to build, and was completed by Roman Emperor Hadrian. (p90)

Panathenaic Stadium Monumental stadium that held ancient contests, Roman sacrifices and, more recently, the first modern Olympics. (p94)

Roman Sites

Odeon of Herodes Atticus This magnificent venue on the south slope of the Acropolis is still used for summer festivals, concerts and plays. (p28)

Tower of the Winds The Roman Agora holds the beautifully carved octagonal tower with functions from weathervane to sundial. (Pictured, left; p48)

Hadrian's Library Once the most opulent structure in Athens, erected around AD 132, it had an internal courtyard and pool bordered by 100 columns. (p50)

Hadrian's Arch Emperor Hadrian's monument commemorating the completion of the Temple of Olympian Zeus and marking the border between old and new. (p91)

Byzantine Sites

Little Metropolis From the 12th century, this church incorporates fragments of a classical frieze in Pentelic marble. (p48)

Church of Kapnikarea The charming 11th-century church sits stranded, smack in the middle of downtown Athens. (p48)

Best
Museums

With the embarrassment of riches that is Athens' and Greece's history, museums are superb showcases of all things Greek. On a short visit you'll have to choose among them, but you won't be disappointed no matter where you go.

Archaeological Museums

Many of Greece's most precious statues and artefacts have been collected in Athens for their own protection. In well-lit, temperature-controlled environments these treasures will be able to survive millennia more. The powerhouse is the National Archaeological Museum, the world's best repository of ancient Greek art and artefacts. The Acropolis Museum, opened to much-deserved fanfare in 2009, is a splendid example of showcasing ancient art in an innovative, modern setting.

Art Museums

Most of Athens' archaeological museums could equally be characterised as art museums, with their troves of Greek and Roman sculptures, pottery and jewellery. But the city also has several museums dedicated to more modern forms: painting, etching, contemporary art forms such as installations, and rotating exhibitions of international shows. They also often have educational programs and lecture or music series from time to time.

Cultural Museums

Some museums, particularly in the Plaka and Monastiraki neighbourhoods, focus on more traditional Greek culture. From puppet making to regional dress and musical instruments – pick your poison. The annexes of the Benaki Museum display everything from Greek and Islamic culture to modern art.

☑ Top Tips

▶ Bring ID to qualify for student, senior citizen or EU discounts.

▶ For the most popular museums, try to go early to beat the crowds.

Archaeological Museums

National Archaeological Museum The world's foremost repository of ancient Greek artefacts in an enormous neoclassical building. (Pictured, above; p100)

Acropolis Museum Art and finds from the Acropolis shine in this spacious, superbly curated gem. (p30)

Stoa of Attalos (p41), Ancient Agora Museum

Museum of Cycladic Art
Equally an art museum,
with minimalist, ancient
Cycladic sculptures that
inspired Picasso and
Modigliani. (p83)

Ancient Agora Museum
Study the history of
democracy and Athenian
civic life. (p41)

Cultural Museums

Benaki Museum This
expansive private collec-
tion brings together pre-
cious works from all over
Greece and the Ottoman
Empire. (p76)

Museum of Islamic Art
A Benaki annexe housing
exquisite examples of
Islamic art and culture.
(p129)

Kanellopoulos Museum
Peruse everything from
vases to icons and jewel-
lery in a Plaka mansion.
(p64)

Greek Folk Art Museum
The main site and its an-
nexes put Greek secular
and religious art on
show: from embroidery
to pottery, weaving and
puppets. (p66)

Jewish Museum A small,
beautifully displayed
collection tracing the history of Greece's Jewish
population. (p64)

Art Museums

**Benaki Museum Pireos
Annexe** One of the city's
leading contemporary
powerhouses in a cool
converted industrial
space. (p129)

**Byzantine & Christian
Museum** Is it art? Is
it culture? It's simply
downright beautiful.
(p82)

**National Museum of
Contemporary Art** In a
freshly remodelled brew-
ery, see contemporary
Greek and international
art stars. (p33)

National Art Gallery
A rambling collection
of predominantly 20th-
century art, emphasising
Greek painters. (p83)

**Theocharakis Foun-
dation for the Fine
Arts & Music** Rotating
exhibitions cycle through
this Kolonaki mansion
that also offers concert
series. (p84)

Best
Food

Traditional Greek cuisine is all about fresh ingredients. Seasonal produce, just-caught seafood, regional ingredients and cooking styles, simple flavours and minimal dressings bring out the flavours of the Mediterranean. And everything is made tastier by this year's olive oil and a crusty loaf of fresh bread.

Styles of Eateries

Greeks love to eat out, and dining is a rowdy, drawn-out, communal affair with friends and family. Despite the proliferation of upscale trendy restaurants, the most popular dining venue is the trusty taverna. Most serve a combination of *mayirefta* (oven-baked or casserole-style dishes) and *tis oras* (made-to-order meat and seafood grills).

The mezes-style of dining – usually at a *mezedhopoleio* (a restaurant specialising in mezedhes) – is very popular, with small dishes shared over long and merry meals – a variation is the *ouzerie*, where ouzo traditionally helped rinse the palate between mezes tastes.

A *psistaria* is a taverna that specialises in grilled meats with a limited menu of salads and starters.

Souvlaki is still Greece's favourite fast food, both the *gyros* (meat slithers cooked on a vertical rotisserie) and skewered-meat versions wrapped in pitta bread, with tomato, onion and lashings of tzatziki.

Trends

Postmodern tavernas or restaurants (*estiatorio*) with a new generation of classically trained chefs redefine the classics to create modern Greek food. Some add a fusion of styles, from Asia to France; regional cuisine is also prized.

☑ Top Tips

▶ Greeks eat late (tourist-friendly eateries open earlier). Typically lunch starts around 2pm and dinner 9pm to 10pm; it's not uncommon for tables to be full at midnight. Tavernas are often open all day.

▶ Athens' seasonal dining scene means many restaurants close for summer, often moving to sister restaurants on the islands or shore.

Making souvlaki, Thanasis (p52)

Best Tavernas

Café Avyssinia A bit like a bistro, with super Acropolis views from upstairs. (p51)

Akordeon Combine top eats with live local music (p51)

Oikeio Top golden ambience, and some international dishes too. (p79)

Kanella Fresh and fab in Gazi. (p130)

Paradosiako Plainly one of Plaka's best. (p68)

Filippou Kolonaki's venerable eatery. (p79)

Best Mezedhes

Tzitzikas & Mermingas Colourful, central and decadent. (p67)

Mavro Provato Join the crowd of locals in Pangrati. (p95)

Filistron Sweeping Acropolis views from the roof terrace. (p119)

Best Haute Cuisine

Funky Gourmet Top gastronomic creations, yet thoroughly Greek. (p126)

Spondi Greco-French top of the tops. (p95)

Aleria Mediterranean menu in a restored mansion. (p127)

2 Mazi Plaka's elegant eatery. (p67)

Mani Mani Regional treats from Mani. (p35)

Best Souvlaki

Kostas Eat standing near the flower market. (p45)

Kalamaki Kolonaki Watch the swanky set stroll. (p85)

Thanasis In the heart of Monastiraki's souvlaki strip. (p52)

Best Local

Diporto Agoras Unmarked, down a flight of stairs near the Central Market. (p57)

Kalnterimi Superfresh home cooking. (p67)

Kimatothrafstis Tiny and relaxed in Exarhia. (p109)

Best Veg-Organic

Avocado From organic to vegan. (p61)

Pure Bliss Lives up to its name. (p67)

Nice N' Easy Has a super weekend brunch. (p85)

Best
Cafes

One favoured Athenian (and Greek) pastime is going for a coffee. Athens' ubiquitous and inevitably packed cafes have Europe's most expensive coffee (between €3 and €5). But with that premium you're essentially hiring the chair, and can linger for hours, watching the cafe action and, alfresco in summer, the passers-by. Some museums also have lovely cafes. And the traditional *kafeneio* (coffee house) can still be found. A *kafeneio* serves Greek coffee, spirits and little else (though in rural villages it may serve food), and remains largely the domain of men.

RUTH ENGEL/LONELY PLANET ©

☑ Top Tip

▶ If you order Greek coffee, it is traditionally brewed in a *briki* (narrow-top pot) and served in a small cup. Let it settle, and then sip it slowly until you reach the muddy grounds at the bottom (don't drink them). It's quite tasty when ordered *metrios* (medium, with one sugar).

Best Cafes

Tailor Made Hip microroastery with tea, sandwiches, desserts and a young Athenian crowd. (p45)

Melina Decked out in homage to Melina Mercouri and one of Plaka's few low-key haunts. (p60)

Da Capo The Kolonaki flagship cafe, anchoring the square – it's *the* place to be seen. (p78)

Filion Writers and the intellectual set gravitate here, in Kolonaki. (p85)

Petite Fleur Sweet, like a French cafe, with enormous, steaming cappuccinos. (p85)

Odeon Cafe Mets' corner coffee shop – a great local hang-out. (p96)

Floral On the square in Exarhia, with a bookshop. (p104)

Best Teahouses

To Tsai Calming and all-natural, from tea to decor. (p86)

Peonia Herbs On a side street in Thisio with high ceilings and countless brews. (p121)

Best Museum Cafes

Benaki Museum Great food in an open dining room, with National Gardens and Acropolis views. (p77)

Acropolis Museum Superb views across the way to the Acropolis. (p30)

Theocharakis Foundation for the Fine Arts & Music A pleasant cafe. (p84)

Best
Tours & Courses

CitySightseeing Athens (☎ 210 921 4174; www.city-sightseeing.com; Plateia Syntagmatos, Syntagma; adult/child €18/8; ⊙every 30min 9am-9pm Apr-Oct, to 6.30pm Nov-Mar; Ⓜ Syntagma) Open-top double-decker buses cruise around town on a 90-minute circuit starting at Syntagma. A 70-minute circuit goes to Piraeus (adult/child €22/9). You can get on and off at 15 stops on a 48-hour ticket.

Hop In Sightseeing (☎ 210 428 5500; www.hopin.com; Leoforos Vasilissis Amalias 44, Makrygianni; ⊙6.30am-10pm; Ⓜ Akropoli) One of three bus companies (including CHAT and Go Tours) running almost identical air-conditioned coach tours in Athens, the Peloponnese and Delphi.

This Is My Athens (http://myathens.thisisathens.org) Volunteer program that pairs you with a local to show you around for two hours. You must book online 72 hours ahead.

Athens: Adventures (☎ 210 922 4044; www.athensadventures.gr) Based at Athens Backpackers; offers a €6 Athens walking tour and day trips to Nafplio, Delphi and Sounio.

Alternative Athens (☎ 6948405242; www.alternative-athens.com) Experience-based tours and workshops to get off the beaten path – from food to street art and bar-hopping.

Trekking Hellas (☎ 210 331 0323; www.trekking.gr; Gounari 96, Marousi) Vast array of activities tours, ranging from Athens walking tours (€50) to caving, cycling, or trekking in the Peloponnese and the islands.

Solebike (☎ 210 921 5620; www.solebike.eu; Lembesi 11, Makrygianni; ⊙9am-3pm Mon-Sat, also 6-8.30pm Tue, Thu & Fri; Ⓜ Akropoli) Hires out electric bikes and offers tours.

Athens Segway Tours (☎ 210 322 2500; www.athenssegwaytours.com; Es-

chinou 9, Plaka; 2hr tour €59; Ⓜ Akropoli) Zip through town on a Segway.

Planet Blue Dive Centre (☎ 210 418 0174; www.planetblue.gr; Velpex Factory, Lavrio; dives €35-80, PADI certification from €300) Popular with seasoned divers, but caters to all levels at sites around Cape Sounion.

☑ **Top Tip**

▶ Limited time to hit the islands? You can take a day cruise from Piraeus to Aegina, Poros and Hydra with **Athens One Day Cruise** (www.athensonedaycruise.com), or choose one Saronic island, and hop on **Hellenic Seaways** (www.hsw.gr) to get there.

Best
With Kids

Best Museums

Hellenic Children's Museum ([☎]210 331 2995; www.hcm.gr; Kydathineon 14, Plaka; admission free; [⏰]10am-2pm Tue-Fri, to 3pm Sat & Sun; [Ⓜ]Syntagma)
More of a play centre, with a games room and 'exhibits', such as a mock-up of a metro tunnel, for children to explore. Workshops range from baking to bubble-making.

Museum of Greek Children's Art ([☎]210 331 2621; www.childrensart museum.gr; Kodrou 9, Plaka; admission €2; [⏰]10am-2pm Tue-Sat, 11am-2pm Sun, closed Aug; [Ⓜ]Syntagma)
Has a room where children can let loose their creative energy, or learn about ancient Greece.

Other Attractions

Hellenic Cosmos ([☎]212 254 0000; www.hellenic-cosmos.gr; Pireos 254, Tavros; per show adult €5-10, child €3-8, day pass adult/child €15/12; [⏰]10am-3pm

Mon-Fri & Sun, closed 2 weeks mid-Aug; [Ⓜ]Kalithea) Take an interactive virtual-reality tour of ancient Greece, about 2km south-west of the city centre.

Planetarium ([☎]210 946 9600; www.eugenfound. edu.gr; Leoforos Syngrou 387, Palio Faliro; adult €6-8, child €4-5; [⏰]5.30-8.30pm Wed-Fri, 10.30am-8.30pm Sat & Sun, closed mid-Jul-late Aug; [Ⓜ]Syngrou-Fix, [🚌]550 or B2 to Onassio) Offers 3D virtual trips to the galaxy, IMAX movies and other high-tech shows. Narration in English (€1).

Attica Zoological Park ([☎]210 663 4724; www. atticapark.gr; Yalou, Spata; adult/child €15/11; [⏰]9am-sunset) Collection of big cats, birds, reptiles etc. Near the airport. Take bus 319 from Doukissis Plakentias metro station.

Allou Fun Park & Kidom ([☎]210 425 6999; www.allou. gr; cnr Leoforos Kifisou & Petrou Rali, Renti; admission free, rides €2-4; [⏰]5-11pm

Mon-Fri, 10am-midnight Sat & Sun; [Ⓜ]Egaleo, [🚌]703, 801, 802, 803, 804, 829, 845 or 909 to Nekrotafio) Further afield is Allou Fun Park, Athens' biggest amusement park complex. Kidom is aimed at younger children. Take a bus from Egaleo metro station.

Best
Bars

Come nightfall, Athens is one of Europe's liveliest capitals. A heady cocktail of the hedonistic Greek spirit, restless energy and relaxed drinking laws add to the city's vibrant nightlife. Athens' bar scene includes anything from glamorous cocktail bars and hip, arty hangouts to casual neighbourhood haunts.

MEXAS/GETTY IMAGES ©

By Neighbourhood

Bars open and close constantly: recent hot pots fill streets around Plateia Karytsi north of Syntagma and Plateia Agia Irini in Monastiraki. Keramikos and Psyrri have seen a recent surge, while Gazi retains a strong nightlife district. Alternative-music clubs and crowded, cheap student bars dot Exarhia, while Kolonaki's scene steadfastly attracts the trendier set.

Best Cocktail Bars

Baba Au Rum Dream it up and they can make it. (p53)

Gin Joint Too many gins to count. (p61)

MoMix Molecular mixology indeed! (p127)

Best Local Bars

Seven Jokers Central, and great to start the night. (p68)

Clumsies Packed, lively and with the buzz of the new. (p68)

Rock'n'Roll Dependably busy, with a casual-chic crowd. (p79)

Hoxton Boho meets celebrity hang-out. (p131)

Alexandrino Classic Exarhia wine bar with great cocktails too. (p109)

Best Speciality Ambience

Blue Fox Rockabilly and '50s-era swing, complete with poodle skirts. (p109)

Brettos Colourful glass-bottle-lined distillery. (p69)

☑ **Top Tips**

▶ Bars often don't kick off until 11pm or midnight.

▶ Sky bars, including Hotel Grande Bretagne's bar, or Galaxy Bar atop the Hilton, offer WOW panoramic views (and prices).

▶ With the current strapped financial climate in Athens, watch your back.

Best Rooftop Terraces

Gazarte Views from Technopolis to the Acropolis. (p127)

Bios Bauhaus arts centre with great rooftop bar. (p127)

Best
Nightlife &
Entertainment

Athens has a thriving live-music scene in winter, with the gamut of Greek music from the popular soulful Greek blues (*rembetika*) to jazz, rock and touring international artists. In summer live music is confined to festivals and outdoor concerts. The full range of symphony, opera and theatre is also on offer.

Greek Music & Bouzoukia

Athens has some of the best *rembetika* in intimate, evocative venues. Most close May to September, so in summer try live-music tavernas around Plaka and Psyrri. Performances usually include both *rembetika* and *laïka* (urban popular music), start at around 11.30pm, and do not have a cover charge, though drinks can be expensive.

High-end *bouzoukia* are expensive extravaganzas, like a circus for grown-ups. Top Greek singers book in for a season and are accompanied by costumed dancers and even contortionists. Dress to impress and prepare to dance till dawn. Check listings for what's on.

Cinema & Theatre

An unforgettable Athens experience is a summer's night at one of the outdoor cinemas or theatres. The main summer happening is the **Hellenic Festival** (Athens & Epidavros Festival; www.greekfestival.gr; 🕐 Jun-Aug), with stagings at the historic Odeon of Herodes Atticus and other venues.

☑ Top Tips

▶ English-language entertainment information appears daily in the Kathimerini supplement in the *International Herald Tribune*; *Athens Plus* also has listings.

▶ Athens tourism site www.breathtaking athens.gr has comprehensive event listings.

▶ Visit www.el culture.gr for arts and culture listings.

Thission open-air cinema (p121)

Best Live Music

Half Note Jazz Club The city's premier jazz venue. (p96)

AN Club Eclectic range of acts in Exarhia. (p111)

Fuzz International acts that attract a younger set. (p133)

Best Rembetika

Stoa Athanaton Legendary club occupying a hall above the central meat market. (p57)

Kavouras Above a souvlaki joint in Exarhia. (p111)

Best Music Tavernas

Akordeon Friendly hosts serve delicious local eats and get the whole place dancing with their songs. (p51)

Perivoli tou Ouranou Old-style taverna with live music in Plaka. (p70)

Palea Plakiotiki Taverna Stamatopoulos Another one of Plaka's busy spots. (p71)

Best Dance

Dora Stratou Dance Theatre Traditional Greek dances alfresco. (p121)

Best Open-Air Cinemas

Dexameni Kolonaki's sweet cinema, surrounded by gardens. (Pictured; left; p79)

Aigli Cinema Zappeio Gardens' fresh-aired spot. (p97)

Thission In Thisio, with Acropolis views. (p121)

Worth a Trip

The city's state-of-the-art concert hall, **Megaron Mousikis** (p34) presents a rich winter program of operas and concerts featuring world-class international and Greek performers. Its Mediterranean restaurant, Fuga, fills an attached garden.

Cine Paris Smack in the middle of Plaka, with some Acropolis views. (p70)

Best
Gay & Lesbian

For the most part Athens' gay and lesbian scene is relatively low-key, though the Athens Pride (www.athenspride.eu) march, held in June, has been an annual event since 2005, with celebrations centred on Plateia Klafthmonos. For nightlife, a new breed of gay and gay-friendly clubs have opened around town, especially in Gazi, but also in Makrygianni, Psyrri, Metaxourghio and Exarhia.

GEORGIOS MAKKAS/ALAMY ©

Best City Centre

Sodade In Gazi; tiny, sleek and superfun for dancing – it draws a great crowd. (p127)

Rooster Cafe and cocktails in the centre of Monastiraki's booming scene, on Plateia Agia Irini. (p53)

S-cape Stays packed with the younger crowd and schedules myriad theme nights. (Pictured, above; p132)

Noiz Club Also in Gazi, for women. (p127)

Lamda Club Busy, three levels and not for the faint of heart. (p37)

BIG The hub of Athens' lively bear scene. (p132)

Magaze This gay-friendly all-day hang-out is a cafe by day and becomes a lively bar after sunset. (p53)

Moe Club A late-night stop in Gazi. (p132)

Best Worth a Trip

Myrovolos (📞210 522 8806; www.facebook.com/ myrovolos; Giatrakou 12; ⏲11am-late daily) In Metaxourgio, this cafe-bar-restaurant is a popular lesbian spot. Greek meals range from €16 to €20.

Koukles (📞694 755 7443; www.facebook.com/Koukles clubathens; Zan Moreas 32; ⏲midnight-4am) In Koukaki, the drag show here rocks.

☑ Top Tips

▶ Check out www. athensinfoguide. com or a copy of the *Greek Gay Guide* booklet at *periptera* (newspaper kiosks).

▶ Gazi has become Athens' gay and lesbian hub, with a gay triangle emerging near the railway line on Leoforos Konstantinoupoleos and Megalou Alexandrou.

Limanakia This popular gay beach is below the rocky coves near Varkiza. Take the tram or A2/E2 express bus to Glyfada, then bus 117 or 122 to the Limnakia B stop.

Best
Art Events & Galleries

Recent years have brought a burgeoning of the arts scene. Even as Athens struggles with other aspects of political or social life, Greece's musicians, performing artists and visual artists remain hard at work and a new breed of multi-use gallery has sprung up to host all of the disciplines. Some feel like museums, others more like nightclubs, and for others it just depends what time of day it is.

MILAN GONDA/SHUTTERSTOCK ©

Best Art Events

Art-Athina (www.art-athina.gr) International contemporary-art fair in May.

Athens Biennial (www.athensbiennial.org) Every two years from June to October.

ReMap (www.remap.org) Parallel event to the Biennial, exhibiting in abandoned buildings.

Documenta 14 (www.documenta.de) The 2017 presentation of Documenta 14 will take place in both Kassel, Germany (as usual), and Athens.

Best Art Galleries

AD Gallery One of Psyrri's best for contemporary art. (p45)

Bernier/Eliades Venerable gallery in Thisio. (p119)

Qbox Gallery Young, emerging local and visiting artists on the international scene. (p57)

Andreas Melas & Helena Papadopoulos Gallery Formerly the AMP Gallery, this gallery merges the efforts of two of Athens' contemporary-art powerhouses. (p57)

CAN Creative contemporary art in Kolonaki. (p84)

Medusa Art Gallery Excellent Greek contemporary painting, sculpture, installations and photography. (p79)

Best Art Shops

Zoumboulakis Gallery Limited-edition prints and posters by leading Greek artists. (p72)

El.Marneri Galerie Local modern art and super jewellery. (p37)

Best Multiuse Spaces

Taf Exhibitions, bar-cafe, cinema and theatre in interesting crumbling historic building. (p51)

Six DOGS Gregarious and central – bar, cafe, music venue and theatre. (p45)

Bios Industrial chic with a cinema, a gallery, a bar and more. (p127)

Technopolis City's art complex in the converted gasworks. (Pictured, above; p130)

Best
Shopping

As with any capital city, the number and array of stores in Athens is rather mind-boggling. Major retail development throughout Athens had seen a swath of new places opening downtown and the city's first major shopping mall launched in the northern suburbs, but the recent economic problems have reversed that trend. Now, look for independent, creative shops that epitomise Athenian ingenuity.

KEN WELSH/GETTY IMAGES ©

Shopping Districts

The most concentrated high-street shopping is on pedestrianised Ermou, which must have more shoes per square metre than anywhere in the world, as well as most of the leading local, European- and global brands. The Citylink complex houses the Attica department store and is the gateway to the top international designers and big-name jewellers along Voukourestiou, leading to the chic designer boutiques throughout Kolonaki.

Plaka (with main shopping streets Kydathineon and Adrianou; pictured, above) and Monastiraki (with its enormous flea market) are the places for souvenirs, from kitsch statues and leather sandals to jewellery and antiques. Exarhia is the place for more eclectic items, from comics to goth clothing and vinyl. Outlying suburbs Kifisia and Glyfada also offer great shopping, in a more relaxed environment.

Find a delectable array of food and spices at the colourful Central Market (p56), and all manner of housewares in the surrounding streets.

☑ **Top Tip**

▶ Sale times (July to August and January to February) offer some great bargains.

▶ Haggling is only acceptable (and effective) in smaller, owner-run souvenir and jewellery stores (especially for cash).

Best Food & Drink Shops

To Pantopoleion Full range of Greek goods near the Central Market. (p57)

Gusto di Grecia Fom cheese to local honeys, cold cuts, olive oil and wine, in Kolonaki. (p87)

Thymari Tou Strefi Exarhia's go-to shop for local foods. (p111)

Aristokratikon Chocoholics' paradise. (p61)

Mastiha Shop All things made from mastic (the sap from Chios). (p61)

Cellier Wine shop extraordinaire. (p73)

Bakaniko Local life in Pangrati: from soup to nuts. (p97)

Best Fashion & Shoes

Ioanna Kourbela Young designer of clothes with flowing lines, in the heart of Plaka. (p61)

Parthenis A father-daughter team design in natural fibres and colours. (p79)

Vassilis Zoulias Supercool couture clothes and shoes with prices to match. (p87)

Rien Hip Gazi atelier for womenswear and sumptuous leather bags. (p133)

Spiliopoulos Bargain hunters galore come for clothes and accessories. There are two branches. (p54)

Kalogirou Shoe heaven in Kolonaki. (p87)

Olgianna Melissinos Handmade bags and Greek-style leather sandals. (p53)

Melissinos Art Olgianna's brother makes great sandals too. (p54)

Best Jewellery

Fanourakis Original, exquisite designs with a minimalist modern bent. Also has a moderately priced line. (p86)

Elena Votsi Contemporary, expensive but oh-so-beautiful. (p87)

Lalaounis Renowned jeweller inspired by Greek history. (p33)

Actipis Low-key sea-pebble and leather jewellery. (p72)

Best Crafts

Forget Me Not All locally designed cool gifts. (p61)

Martinos Selling Greek antiques of all sorts since 1890. (p54)

Aidini Artisanal metal creations from mirrors to candlesticks. (p71)

Best Local Shop

Mompso Shop for everything from brass sheep's bells to shepherds' crooks and horse headdresses. (p45)

Best Cosmetics

Korres Greece's premier organic-beauty product company. (p71)

Apivita This natural beauty line in Kolonaki also has an express spa. (p86)

Sabater Hermanos All-natural soaps and bath crystals in Psyrri. (p55)

Best Music Shop

Xylouris Run by a famous Cretan musical family, and a font of information on Greek music. (p72)

John Samuelin Instruments and recordings, too. (p55)

Best Bazaars

Monastiraki Flea Market A daily extravaganza, not to be missed. (p45)

Athens Central Market Feed your eyes with all the sights at this expansive food market and its surrounding streets. (p56)

Best
For Free

Athens is not a particularly expensive city to begin with, but every euro counts and there are still some super sights for free. Simply wandering the downtown and taking in the bustling city streets and markets, plus ancient sites visible from the street, can fill a visit.

LONELY PLANET/GETTY IMAGES ©

Best Free Museums

Benaki Museum The top-notch main building (*not* the annexes) is free on Thursdays. (p76)

Museum of Greek Popular Instruments Displays and recordings of a wide selection of traditional instruments and costumes. (Pictured, above) (p66)

Epigraphical Museum The most significant collection of Greek inscriptions on a veritable library of stone tablets. (p107)

Best Free to Explore

Filopappou Hill Historic hill strewn with ancient ruins, with some of the best Acropolis views. (p114)

National Gardens Lush sanctuary with a playground and small zoo. (p64)

Athens Central Market Roam through stacks of tomatoes, rows of butchered lambs, piles of raw spices. (p56)

Monastiraki Flea Market Hodgepodge of souvenir and bric-a-brac shops. (p45)

Best Free Sites

Aristotle's Lyceum Aristotle taught rhetoric and philosophy at this ancient site. (p82)

Roman Baths Excavated during the metro build; they are easy to see alongside the National Gardens. (p95)

Syntagma Metro station dig The ancient aqueduct and unearthed artefacts are on display at the metro station.

Turkish Baths In Plaka, two sites remain, one inside the gift shop of the Museum of Greek Popular Instruments. (p50)

☑ **Top Tips**

▶ Archaeological sites, such as the Acropolis, Temple of Olympian Zeus, Ancient Agora, Roman Agora and Keramikos, are not only included in the €12 Acropolis joint ticket, but are free on the first Sunday of the month from November to March, and on certain holidays.

▶ Sights such as Hadrian's Arch (p91) and the Panathenaic Stadium (p94) are easy to observe from the street.

Byzantine churches All over, they give a glimpse into the heart of Byzantium.

Survival Guide

Survival Guide

Before You Go

When to Go

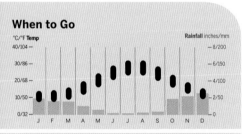

°C/°F Temp
Rainfall inches/mm
40/104 —
— 8/200
30/86 —
— 6/150
20/68 —
— 4/100
10/50 —
— 2/50
0/32 —
— 0
J F M A M J J A S O N D

→ Summer (Jun–Aug)
Blazing hot. Peak accommodation prices. Athenians leave in August; some restaurants, galleries and bars close. This also applies to Easter.

→ Autumn (Sep) Temperatures mild, crowds have thinned. Accommodation prices can drop by 20%.

→ Winter (Oct–Mar)
Temperatures drop; occasional snow. Athens nightlife booms. Accommodation at its cheapest. Ferry schedules skeletal.

→ Spring (Apr–May) Like autumn, temperatures are mild; few crowds. Accommodation prices around 20% less than summer.

Book Your Stay

→ Plaka and Monastiraki are the most popular places for travellers and have a choice of accommodation across the price spectrum. These are the premier sightseeing neighbourhoods.

→ Many high-end hotels are around Syntagma.

→ Some excellent pensions and midrange hotels dot the area south of the Acropolis, around the quiet neighbourhood of Makrygianni.

→ Around Omonia some hotels have been upgraded, but there is still a general seediness that detracts from the area, especially at night.

→ The best rooms in Athens fill up quickly in July and August; book ahead.

→ Most places offer considerable discounts, especially in the low season, for longer stays and online bookings.

→ No-smoking rules are only occasionally enforced.

→ For longer stays or if you're travelling with the family, a furnished studio or apartment may offer better value than some of the budget hotels.

Useful Websites

Lonely Planet (www.lonelyplanet.com/Greece/Athens) Find reviews and book online.

Boutique Athens (www.boutiqueathens.com) Book ahead for a superbly renovated, spacious apartment or whole house, with locations all over town.

Athens Studios (www.athensstudios.gr) Comfortable, modern apartments near the Acropolis.

AthenStyle (www.athenstyle.com) Well-equipped studios; balconies have Acropolis views.

EP16 (www.ep16.com) Renovated, spacious apartments; the roof garden has Acropolis views. Also apartments in Gazi.

Best Budget

Hotel Cecil (www.cecilhotel.gr) Charming old-style hotel with high ceilings and simple rooms.

City Circus (www.citycircus.gr) Bright, well-designed rooms with modern bathrooms are configured as dorms or private rooms, some with kitchens.

Athens Backpackers (www.backpackers.gr) From dorm rooms to studio apartments, with a smile and loads of fun.

AthenStyle (www.athenstyle.com) Bright, arty hostel with some Acropolis views.

Hotel Phaedra (www.hotelphaedra.com) Many of the rooms at this small, family-run hotel have balconies overlooking a church or the Acropolis.

Tempi Hotel (www.tempihotel.gr) Small, but some rooms have balconies overlooking Agia Irini.

Best Midrange

Hera Hotel (www.herahotel.gr) Classic elegance within spitting distance of the Acropolis.

Herodion (www.herodion.gr) Business cool in quiet Makrygianni.

Sweet Home Hotel (www.thesweethomehotel.com) Small, boutique hotel just a stone's throw from all the major Athens sights.

Central Hotel (www.centralhotel.gr) Sleek rooms in the middle of Plaka.

Periscope (www.yeshotels.gr) Mod pods in chic Kolonaki.

Adonis Hotel (www.hotel-adonis.gr) Friendly staff, tidy rooms and Acropolis-view breakfast room in central Plaka.

Best Top End

Electra Palace (www.electrahotels.gr) Plaka's most luxurious, with great food and service to match.

NEW Hotel (www.yeshotels.gr) Style, style, style at this central design hotel.

Hotel Grande Bretagne (www.grandebretagne.gr) The venerable hotel of royalty and stars, towering over Plateia Syntagmatos.

Athens Gate (www.athensgate.gr) Dramatic views of Temple of Olympian Zeus at this business hotel.

Ochre & Brown (www.oandbhotel.com) Subtle, suave boutique hotel at the intersection of Psyrri, Monastiraki and Thisio.

Arriving in Athens

☑ **Top Tip** For the best way to get to your accommodation, see p17.

Eleftherios Venizelos International Airport

➡ Half-hourly blue-line metro trains (one way/ return €8/14, one hour) run between the city centre and airport from 5.30am to 11.30pm.

➡ When returning to the airport some trains terminate early at Doukissis Plakentias, where you get out and wait till an airport train (displayed on the train and platform screen) comes along.

➡ Express bus X95 (€5, one to 1½ hours) operate every 20 minutes, 24 hours a day, between the airport and Plateia Syntagmatos (Syntagma Sq), with a few intermediate stops. Buy tickets at the kiosk near the bus stop.

➡ Taxis (www.athens airporttaxi.com) to the city centre cost a flat fare day/night (midnight to 5am) €35/50 (one hour).

➡ Express bus X96 (€5, 1½ hours) operate 24 hours (every 20 minutes) from the airport to Piraeus, the main port.

Piraeus Port

➡ Metro trains (€1.20, green line) run to the city

Tickets & Passes

Tickets are good for 70 minutes (€1.20) and 24-hour/five-day travel passes (€4/10) are valid for all forms of public transport except for airport services, the three-day tourist ticket (€20) includes one round-trip airport transport. Bus/ trolleybus-only tickets (€1.20) cannot be used on the metro. Children under six travel free; passengers under 18 and over 65 pay half-fare. Buy tickets in metro stations or transport kiosks or most *periptera* (newspaper kiosks). Validate the ticket in the machine as you board your transport of choice.

centre every half-hour from 5.30am to 11.30pm.

➡ Taxis to the city centre cost €15 to €30 (30 to 45 minutes).

➡ Bus 040 (€1.20) runs to Syntagma every 15 to 20 minutes.

➡ Athens tramway and additional metro extensions to the port of Piraeus are underway, and scheduled to be completed by 2017.

Getting Around

Metro

☑ **Best for...**almost all daytime travel; there's an extensive network of conveniently located stations.

➡ The metro (www. ametro.gr) runs every three to 10 minutes from 5.30am to just after midnight (to 2am Friday and Saturday).

➡ Tickets (€1.20) must be validated at platform entrances and are valid for 70 minutes on all modes of transport.

➡ The three intersecting lines are: green (line 1, also known as the Ilektriko), red (line 2) and blue (line 3).

➡ All stations have wheelchair access.

Taxi

☑ **Best for...**quick trips around town with loads of luggage, and night-time travel.

➡ Despite the large number of yellow taxis, it can be tricky getting one

specially during rush
our. Thrust your arm out
igorously.

To avoid an argument
bout the fare, check that
he meter is running and
et to the correct tariff and
xpect airport, toll and bag
ver 10kg) surcharges.
otal fares vary depending
n traffic.

If a taxi picks you up
hile already carrying
assengers, the fare is
ot shared: each person
ays the fare on the meter
inus any diversions to
rop others (note what it's
t when you get in).

• Short trips around cen-
al Athens cost around
5. Beware of taxi scams.

• The Uber smartphone
pp (www.uber.com) is in
ffect in Athens.

• Taxibeat (www.taxibeat.
r) is a mobile app for
ailing available taxis by
ocation and rating. Can
ook from abroad.

• Welcome Pickups
www.welcomepickups.
om) provides prebooked
irport pick-ups and
rop-offs.

eliable Operators
ooking a radio taxi costs
1.92 extra.

thina 1 (📞 210 921 7942)

Enotita (📞 210 645 9000,
18388; www.athensradiotaxi
enotita.gr)

Parthenon (📞 210 581
4711)

Bus & Trolleybus
☑ **Best for...**the airport
after the metro has
stopped running.

➡ For the city centre,
walking, metro and taxis
are almost always better
choices. Buses are better
for areas not reached by
metro.

➡ Athens' overhead cable
trolleybuses run between
5am and midnight and
service much of the city.
Trolleybuses run 24 hours
on the 11–Patisia–Pangrati
route.

Tram
☑ **Best for...**beach-club-
hopping.

➡ Athens' tram (www.stasy.
gr) offers a slow, scenic
coastal journey to Faliro
and Voula, via Glyfada. It's

handy for revellers travelling to the city's beaches
and beach clubs.

➡ The central terminus
is opposite the National
Gardens. Tickets (€1.20)
are purchased on the
platforms.

➡ Trams run from
Syntagma to Faliro (45
minutes), Syntagma to
Voula (one hour) and Faliro
to Voula from 5.30am to
1am Sunday to Thursday
(every 10 minutes), and
from 5.30am to 2.30am
on Friday and Saturday
(every 40 minutes).

Essential Information

Business Hours
☑ **Top Tip** With the odd
economic climate, open-
ing hours and prices are
changing continuously;
some places close. Call
ahead if in doubt.

Transport Maps
Metro maps are quite clear in the stations and on
board trains, but for getting further afield, pick
up maps and timetables at the EOT tourist office
(p165), the airport and train stations, the **Athens
Urban Transport Organisation** (OASA; 📞185;
www.oasa.gr), or from its website.

Money-Saving Tips

➡ Look out for free entry at sights.

➡ Buy the €12 Acropolis ticket (p35) as it includes entry to seven other major archaeological sights.

➡ Carry ID for student, EU or senior-citizen discounts.

➡ Greek taverna portions are large, and meals are often shared family-style – follow this local custom.

220V/50Hz

Standard business hours are as follows, unless specified in the reviews:

Banks 8am to 2.30pm Monday to Thursday, 8am to 2pm Friday

Bars 8pm to late

Cafes 10am to midnight

Central post offices 7.30am to 8pm Monday to Friday, 7.30am to 2pm Saturday, 9am to 1.30pm Sunday

Clubs 10pm to late

Restaurants 1pm to 3pm (lunch) and 7pm to 1am (dinner), though most restaurants in central Athens and tourist areas stay open all day in summer.

Shops 9am to 3pm Monday, Wednesday and Saturday, 9am to 8pm Tuesday, Thursday and Friday. In Plaka and tourist areas some shops stay open until about 11pm in summer. Department stores and supermarkets 8am to 8pm Monday to Friday, 8am to 6pm Saturday.

Electricity

220V/50Hz

Emergencies

Ambulance/first-aid (🕿166)

Police (🕿100)

SOS Doctors (🕿1016, 210 821 1888; ⊙24hr) Pay service with English-speaking doctors.

Tourist police (🕿210 920 0724, 24hr 171; Veïkou 43-45, Koukaki; ⊙8am-10pm; Ⓜ Syngrou-Fix, Akropoli)

Visitor emergency assistance (🕿112) Toll-free 24-hour service in English

Internet Access

→ Most hotels and many cafes have internet access or wi-fi.

→ Free wireless hot spots are at Syntagma, Thisio, Gazi and the port of Piraeus.

→ Buy prepaid dial-up internet cards for your laptop at OTE (Greece's main telecommunications carrier) shops or Germanos stores.

Media

English-language papers are the English edition of *Kathimerini* (www.ekathimerini.com), published daily (except Sunday) with the *International Herald Tribune*, and the weekly *Athens Plus*. **Press Project** (www.thepressproject.gr) has online news with an English version.

Money

☑ **Top Tip** It's wise to keep cash on hand as many establishments prefer it, and bank closures have happened as part of the debt crisis.

ATMs Widely available; usually a charge on withdrawals abroad.

Credit cards Accepted in some hotels, restaurants and shops, but certainly not all.

Currency Greece uses the euro.

Money changers Several around Syntagma, as well as banks.

Tipping Small change and rounding up is customary.

Public Holidays

☑ **Top Tip** Greece's biggest blow-out holiday, Orthodox Easter, is preceded by a week of celebration. The whole country gets a holiday and hotels book up.

All banks and shops and most museums and ancient sites close on public holidays.

New Year's Day 1 January

Epiphany 6 January

First Sunday in Lent February

Greek Independence Day 25 March

Good Friday March/April

Orthodox Easter Sunday 1 May 2016, 16 April 2017, 8 April 2018, 28 April 2019

May Day (Protomagia) 1 May

Whit Monday (Agiou Pnevmatos) 50 days after Easter Sunday

Feast of the Assumption 15 August

Ohi Day 28 October

Christmas Day 25 December

St Stephen's Day 26 December

Safe Travel

→ Crime has increased in Athens with the onset of the financial crisis. Though violent street crime remains relatively rare, travellers should be alert on the streets, especially at night, and beware the issues listed here.

→ Streets surrounding Omonia have become markedly seedier, with an increase in prostitutes and junkies; avoid the area, especially at night.

Strikes

Strikes and demonstrations can disrupt public transport and sight openings, but they are often announced in advance. They usually proceed to Syntagma Square; steer clear. Check www.livingingreece.gr/strikes/ for the latest.

Pickpockets

Favourite hunting grounds are the metro, particularly the Piraeus–Kifisia line, and crowded streets around Omonia, Athinas and the Monastiraki Flea Market.

Taxi Scams

➡ Most (but not all) rip-offs involve taxis picked up from ranks at the airport, train stations, bus terminals and particularly the port of Piraeus. At Piraeus, avoid the drivers at the port exit asking if you need a taxi; hail one off the street.

➡ Some drivers don't turn on the meter and demand whatever they think they can get away with; others claim you gave them a smaller bill than you did and short-change you. Only negotiate a set fare if you have some idea of the cost.

➡ Some drivers may try to persuade you that the hotel you want to go to is full, even if you have a booking.

Bar Scams

➡ Scammers target tourists in central Athens, particularly around Syntagma. One scam goes like this: friendly Greek approaches solo male traveller; friendly Greek reveals that he, too, is from out of town or does the 'I have a cousin in Australia' routine and suggests they go to a bar for a drink. Before they know it women appear, more drinks are ordered and the conman disappears, leaving the traveller to pay an exorbitant bill. Smiles disappear and the atmosphere turns threatening.

➡ Some bars lure intoxicated males with talk of sex and present them with outrageous bills.

➡ Some bars and clubs serve what are locally known as *bombes*, adulterated drinks diluted with cheap illegal imports or methanol-based spirit substitutes. They leave you feeling decidedly low the next day.

Telephone Services

☑ **Top Tip** In Greece all phone numbers have 10 digits. Landline numbers start with '2', mobile numbers start with '6'.

➡ Public telephones are ubiquitous but sometimes out of order, a result of the decline in demand due to the proliferation of mobile phones.

Restaurant Guide

Taverna The classic Greek taverna has a few specialist variations: the *psarotaverna* (serving fish and seafood), and *hasapotaverna* or *psistaria* (for chargrilled or spit-roasted meat).

Mayirio (cookhouse) Specialises in traditional one-pot stews and baked dishes (*mayirefta*).

Estiatorio Serves upmarket international cuisine or Greek classics in a more formal setting.

Mezedhopoleio Offers lots of mezedhes (small plates).

Ouzerie In a similar vein to the *mezedhopoleio*, the *ouzerie* serves mezedhes (traditionally arriving with each round of ouzo).

The phones are easy to operate, take phonecards *telekarta*; available at kiosks and tourist shops), not coins, and can be used for local, long-distance and international calls. The 'i' at the top left of the push-button dialling panel brings up the operating instructions in English.

A local call costs around €0.30 for three minutes. It's also possible to use payphones with a range of discount-card schemes (dial an access code and enter your card number). The OTE version of this is 'Hronokarta'. The cards come with instructions in Greek and English and talk time is enormous compared to standard phonecard rates.

Several mobile service providers offer data and pay-as-you-talk services: buy a rechargeable SIM card and have your own Greek mobile number.

US/Canadian phones need to have a dual- or tri-band system, and will have to be set to roaming, or buy a local mobile and SIM card.

International access code: ☑ 00

Greece country code: ☑ 30

International operator: ☑ 139

Toilets

Public toilets are a rarity, except at airports and bus and train stations. Cafes are the best option, but you'll be expected to buy something for the privilege.

The Greek plumbing system can't handle toilet paper: the pipes are too narrow. Toilet paper etc should be placed in the small bin next to every toilet.

Tourist Information

EOT (Greek National Tourist Organisation; ☑ 210 331 0716, 210 331 0347; www.visitgreece. gr; Dionysiou Areopagitou 18-20, Makrygianni; ☺ 8am-8pm Mon-Fri, 10am-4pm Sat & Sun May-Sep, 9am-7pm Mon-Fri Oct-Apr; M Akropoli) Free Athens map, transport information and *Athens & Attica* booklet. There's also a desk at **Athens Airport** (☑ 9am-5pm Mon-Fri & 10am-4pm Sat).

Athens Airport Information Desk (☺ 24hr) This 24-hour desk has Athens info, booklets and the Athens Spotlighted

discount card for goods and services.

Athens City Information Kiosks (www.breathtaking athens.com) Maps, transport information and all Athens info available through two branches: Acropolis (☑ 210 321 7116; Dionysiou Areopagitou & Leoforos Syngrou; ☺ 9am-9pm May-Sep; M Akropoli) and Airport (☑ 210 353 0390; ☺ 8am-8pm; M Airport).

Travellers with Disabilities

Though some adaptations have been made for wheelchairs, Athens remains a largely inconvenient city for travellers with disabilities. Be specific when booking a hotel to make sure it really can accommodate you.

Visas

EU & Schengen countries No visa required.

Australia, Canada, Israel, Japan, New Zealand and USA No visa required for tourist visits of up to 90 days.

Other countries Check with a Greek embassy or consulate.

Language

Greek is believed to be one of the oldest European languages, with an oral tradition of 4000 years and a written tradition of approximately 3000 years.

The Greek alphabet can look a bit intimidating if you're used to the Roman alphabet, but with a bit of practice you'll start recognising the characters quickly. If you read our pronunciation guides as if they were English, you'll be understood. Stressed syllables are in italics. Note that 'm/f/n' indicates masculine, feminine and neuter forms.

To enhance your trip with a phrasebook, visit **lonelyplanet.com**. Lonely Planet iPhone phrasebooks are available through the Apple App store.

Basics

Hello.

| Γειά σας. | *ya·sas* (polite) |
| Γειά σου. | *ya·su* (informal) |

Good morning/evening.

| Καλή μέρα/σπέρα. | *ka·li me·ra/spe·ra* |

Goodbye.

| Αντίο. | *an·di·o* |

Yes./No.

| Ναι./Οχι. | *ne/o·hi* |

Please.

| Παρακαλώ. | *pa·ra·ka·lo* |

Thank you.

| Ευχαριστώ. | *ef·ha·ri·sto* |

Sorry.

| Συγγνώμη. | *sigh·no·mi* |

What's your name?

| Πώς σας λένε; | *pos sas le·ne* |

My name is ...

| Με λένε ... | *me le·ne ...* |

Do you speak English?

| Μιλάτε αγγλικά; | *mi·la·te an·gli·ka* |

I (don't) understand.

| (Δεν) καταλαβαίνω. | *(dhen) ka·ta·la·ve·no* |

Eating & Drinking

I'd like ...	Θα ήθελα ...	*tha i·the·la ...*
a cup of coffee	ένα φλυτζάνι καφέ	*e·na fli·dza·ni ka·fe*
a table for two	ένα τραπέζι για δύο άτομα	*e·na tra·pe·zi ya dhi·o a·to·m*
one beer	μία μπύρα	*mi·a bi·ra*

I'm a vegetarian.

| Είμαι χορτοφάγος. | *i·me hor·to·fa·ghos* |

What would you recommend?

| Τι θα συνιστούσες; | *ti tha si·ni·stu·ses* |

Cheers!

| Εις υγείαν! | *is i·yi·an* |

That was delicious.

| Ήταν νοστιμότατο. | *i·tan no·sti·mo·ta·to* |

Please bring the bill.

| Το λογαριασμό, παρακαλώ. | *to lo·ghar·ya·zmo pa·ra·ka·lo* |

Shopping

I'd like to buy ...

| Θέλω ν' αγοράσω ... | *the·lo na·gho·ra·so ..* |

I'm just looking.

| Απλώς κοιτάζω. | *ap·los ki·ta·zo* |

How much is it?

| Πόσο κάνει; | *po·so ka·ni* |

It's too expensive.

| Είναι πολύ ακριβό. | *i·ne po·li a·kri·vo* |

Can you lower the price?

Μπορείς να	bo·ris na
κατεβάσεις	ka·te·va·sis
την τιμή;	tin ti·mi

Emergencies

Help!

Βοήθεια!	vo·i·thya

Call a doctor!

Φωνάξτε ένα	fo·nak·ste e·na
γιατρό!	yi·a·tro

Call the police!

Φωνάξτε την	fo·nak·ste tin
αστυνομία!	a·sti·no·mi·a

There's been an accident.

Έγινε ατύχημα.	ey·i·ne a·ti·hi·ma

I'm ill.

Είμαι άρρωστος.	i·me a·ro·stos

It hurts here.

Πονάει εδώ.	po·na·i e·dho

I'm lost

Έχω χαθεί.	e·kho kha·thi

Time & Numbers

What time is it?

Τι ώρα είναι;	ti o·ra i·ne

It's (two o'clock).

Είναι (δύο η ώρα).	i·ne (dhi·o i o·ra)

yesterday	χθες	hthes
today	σήμερα	si·me·ra
tomorrow	αύριο	av·ri·o
morning	πρωί	pro·i
afternoon	απόγευμα	a·po·yev·ma
evening	βράδυ	vra·dhi

1	ένας/μία	e·nas/mi·a (m/f)
	ένα	e·na (n)
2	δύο	dhi·o
3	τρεις	tris (m&f)
	τρία	tri·a (n)
4	τέσσερεις	te·se·ris (m&f)
	τέσσερα	te·se·ra (n)
5	πέντε	pen·de
6	έξη	e·xi
7	επτά	ep·ta
8	οχτώ	oh·to
9	εννέα	e·ne·a
10	δέκα	dhe·ka

Transport & Directions

Where is ...?

Πού είναι ...;	pu i·ne ...

What's the address?

Ποια είναι η	pia i·ne i
διεύθυνση;	dhi·ef·thin·si

Can you show me (on the map)?

Μπορείς να μου	bo·ris na mu
δείξεις (στο χάρτη);	dhik·sis (sto khar·ti)

I want to go to ...

Θέλω να πάω	the·lo na pao
στο/στη ...	sto/sti ...

Where do I buy a ticket?

Πού αγοράζω	pu a·gho·ra·zo
εισιτήριο;	i·si·ti·ri·o

What time does it leave?

Τι ώρα φεύγει;	ti o·ra fev·yi

Does it stop at ...?

Σταματάει στο ...;	sta·ma·ta·i sto ...

I'd like to get off at ...

Θα ήθελα	tha i·the·la na
να κατεβώ ...	na ka·te·vo ...

Behind the Scenes

Send Us Your Feedback

We love to hear from travellers – your comments help make our books better. We read every word, and we guarantee that your feedback goes straight to the authors. Visit **lonelyplanet.com/contact** to submit your updates and suggestions.

Note: We may edit, reproduce and incorporate your comments in Lonely Planet products such as guidebooks, websites and digital products, so let us know if you don't want your comments reproduced or your name acknowledged. For a copy of our privacy policy visit lonelyplanet.com/privacy.

Alexis Averbucks' Thanks

Boundless gratitude to Alexandra Stamopoulou for her INSPIRATION, spot-on recommendations, and her unflagging friendship. She travels with me everywhere. Ryan Ver Berkmoes was, as always, a peachy Athens co-explorer. Applause for Brana: conscientious, informed and compassionate editor. Margarita Kontzia, Kostas and Zisis Karakatsanis, and Anthy and Costas make Athens home for me, and generously share their brilliant knowledge of the city.

Acknowledgments

Cover photograph:
Acropolis; mffoto/Shutterstock ©

Contents photograph pp4–5:
Acropolis; Scott E Barbour/Getty Images ©

This Book

This 3rd edition of Lonely Planet's *Pocket Athens* guidebook was researched and written by Alexis Averbuck. The 1st edition (published as an Encounter guide) was written by Victoria Kyriakopoulos and the 2nd edition by Alexis. This guidebook was produced by the following:

Destination Editor Brana Vladisavljevic **Product Editors** Kate Mathews, Amanda Williamson **Coordinating Editor** Simon Williamson **Book Designer** Wendy Wright **Assisting Book Designer** Virginia Moreno **Senior Cartographer** Valentina Kremenchutskaya **Cartographer** Mick Garrett **Assisting**

Editor Charlotte Orr **Cover Researcher** Naomi Parker **Thanks to** Kate Chapman, Helen Johnson, Andi Jones, Kate Kiely, Sarah Lombard, Claire Murphy, Claire Naylor, Karyn Noble, Lauren O'Connell, Evangelia Papadopoulou, Anthony Phelan, Dianne Schallmeiner, Vicky Smith, Lauren Wellicome, Tony Wheeler

Index

See also separate subindexes for:

🍴 **Eating p173**

🍺 **Drinking p173**

🎭 **Entertainment p174**

🛍 **Shopping p174**

⊗ Eating

⊖ Drinking